HOW TO DEFEAT ALCOHOLISM

HOW TO DEFEAT ALCOHOLISM

*Nutritional Guidelines
for Getting Sober*

JOSEPH D. BEASLEY, M.D.

TIMES BOOKS

RANDOM HOUSE

Grateful acknowledgment is made to Alcoholics Anonymous World Services, Inc., for permission to reprint "The Twelve Steps" and "The Twelve Traditions".

Library of Congress Cataloging-in-Publication Data

Beasley, Joseph D.
How to defeat alcoholism: the new body/mind approach
to treating
alcoholism, codependence, and children of alcoholics
p. cm.
Bibliography: p.
Includes index.
ISBN 0-8129-1807-X :
1. Alcoholism—Popular works. 2. Self-care, Health. I.
Title.
RC565.B37 1989
616.86′1—dc20

Manufactured in the United States of America

9 8 7 6 5 4 3 2

First Edition

TO KIMLEY,
for her love, support,
and the honor she bestowed on me in becoming my wife

ACKNOWLEDGMENTS

My obligations to the individuals and institutions who have contributed to the development of this book are numerous and only partially discharged by this brief expression of appreciation.

- Catherine A. Heusel for the major contribution she made in researching and editing this manuscript
- Frank King, Jerry Swift, Loretta Shum, and Lorraine Miller for their help over the past five years in developing the review of the field of alcoholism on which this manuscript is based
- Drs. Benjamin and Douglas Stein for their support of my work and their foresight and leadership in developing Brunswick House
- Leon Botstein and Dimitri Papadimitriou of the Bard Center for the Bard Fellowship in Medicine and Science
- The staffs of the Medicine and Nutrition Unit, Brunswick House, Brunswick Hall, and the Brunswick Hospital Center for their untiring efforts and the tremendous amount they teach me each day
- The American Society of Addiction Medicine for its leadership in developing the emerging field of addictionology

- The American Medical Association for more than thirty years of efforts in the cause of improving awareness and treatment of alcoholism
- The many patients it has been my privilege to treat for being the best of all teachers

CONTENTS

HOW TO DEFEAT ALCOHOLISM

1
WHY I WROTE THIS BOOK

In 1979, a forty-seven-year-old man took a suite in the penthouse of a Manhattan hotel to work on some personal problems. He was feeling frustrated and hopeless. His idealistic dreams had failed, and he felt completely alienated from a society whose priorities were incomprehensible to him. His depression had deepened over the previous five years, and various therapies and medications had failed to relieve it. So, on a beautiful summer day in 1979, he decided to cure his problems once and for all.

With alcohol.

He checked into his suite with a case of vodka and called down to the desk to say he would be leaving for a few days and request that they take messages. He bolted the door from the inside. And he began to drink his way through the case of vodka.

Time soon lost all significance. He existed in a fog, drifting in and out of reality, finishing several bottles of vodka a day.

As he drank his frustration, anger, and depression grew. So he drank still more.

After several days of this, he became aware of someone knocking at the door. He did not want to be disturbed, so he did not answer. The phone had been ringing earlier, but he had pulled it out of the wall and it had stopped. A while later someone knocked again, but he still did not answer. Shortly after this, he heard someone try a key in the door. He began to get nervous. Someone was going to come and take away the vodka. Someone was going to try to stop him from committing suicide. He stood up groggily.

The next thing he knew, someone battered the door down. Two police officers came in through the shattered door, followed by a woman. It was a woman who loved him very much. She was the one who had been knocking on the door, and eventually had called the police. She knew he was depressed and figured that something was wrong.

The hotel was old, with high ceilings and wide, tall windows. Windows that were easy to jump out of. When the police broke in he ran to an open window and told them not to come any closer or he would jump. They spoke to him gently, as to a child or frightened animal, and edged closer. Finally they lunged for him—just as he threw himself out the window.

One officer caught his left leg and clung to his foot while the other grappled for his flailing right leg. Together they pulled him back in the window. At this point the man became a raving maniac, determined that they were not going to interfere with his suicide. They eventually succeeded in strapping him to a stretcher and transporting him to a psychiatric hospital in Manhattan. He was placed in a psychiatric ward and given medication to calm him down.

He was still thinking clearly enough to hide the medicine in his cheek and spit it out when he was left alone. Then he set about finishing the job he had begun at the hotel.

The only piece of furniture which was not bolted to the floor was a "safety mirror" attached to the wall. Furious, he ripped the mirror out of the wall and used one of the shards to cut his arms. He started bleeding. The crash of the mirror brought people into the room.

After binding his wounds, they put him in a padded cell, with one window set high in the wall behind a steel grate. Once again, he feigned calm and pretended to be going to sleep. When his attendant left he examined the steel grate. One area of the plaster seemed soft, and he worked at it until he was able to pull the grate out of the wall and get at the many-paned window. He lifted himself up to the window and began kicking furiously at the window glass.

Once again he was caught, and this time he was placed in a straitjacket in a padded cell, with a round-the-clock attendant. Drugged and wrapped securely in the heavy canvas straitjacket, he was totally frustrated in his attempts to kill himself, and finally fell into a deep and dreamless sleep.

When he woke, most of the alcohol had cleared from his system, and he began to realize what he had been trying to do. He knew that he no longer wanted to kill himself. He also knew that he was going into withdrawal.

He could feel his pulse racing and was aware of tremors throughout his strapped-down body. He began to sweat and knew that his temperature was becoming elevated. Then he was hit with a watery diarrhea like that in cholera.

The staff, convinced he was no longer suicidal, removed the straitjacket and placed him back in the psychiatric ward. There, he was racked with tremors, and the diarrhea increased. His head ached, and he knew that he was becoming dehydrated. He tried to communicate this to the attendants and nurses, but they ignored his pleas for juices and other liquids as the ravings of a madman.

His frustration and worry were made worse by the fact that he knew exactly what was happening in his body, and the possibly fatal consequences of withdrawal. For this man was a physician, a man well trained in detecting the sort of dangerous electrolyte imbalance that he was developing. He was literally dying, but no one would listen to him.

He finally convinced the charge nurse to get a doctor to see him. The doctor was a young man from the Philippines who spoke little English. The man in withdrawal had done some work in the Philippines, and knew quite a bit about the town where this young doctor was from. He explained this to the doctor, trying to convince him of his sanity. The young doctor was not convinced.

Back on the ward, the man tried to correct his electrolyte imbalance by drinking lots of fluids. He requested more and more fruit juice. The staff began to suspect that he was trying to commit suicide by overdosing on liquids, and began to restrict his fluids! Desperate now, he and another patient broke into the cabinet where the juice was stored and stole about a gallon of fruit juice.

His tremors and diarrhea developed into D.T.'s. He began

to have hallucinations, which he fought to hide lest they think he was really going crazy and restrain him or overmedicate him. It took four days for the D.T.'s to subside. He was lucky that he did not die.

After seven days in the hospital he was placed in group therapy. There, he met a social worker who was willing to listen to him and believe that he was suffering from alcoholism, not insanity, and that he really was a doctor. He convinced her to contact one of the doctors on staff at the hospital whom he had known and worked with since the early sixties. This doctor confirmed his story. After eight days of cold turkey withdrawal from alcohol, he was finally in contact with someone who could help him.

I was that suicidal physician, and it took a brush with death to make me realize that my problem was not depression or disillusionment or frustration with governmental stupidity, but alcoholism. It took eight days of living hell and real terror of impending death. I am writing this book in an effort to keep others from reaching a similar state.

When I was finally released from that psychiatric ward and moved to a more relaxed ward, I delved into every book and paper on alcoholism I could find. It became very clear to me that most treatment programs I was looking at were not adequate to handle the drastic medical needs of an alcoholic like myself. I began to formulate my own ideas for treating alcoholism—ideas that would include both body and mind in the treatment plan. In my search for information, I found out that there was a doctor on Long Island who was working on the problems of addiction and mental illness from a biobehavioral standpoint. I contacted this man, Dr. David Hawkins, at

Brunswick House and asked if he would be willing to treat me. Dr. Hawkins consented.

While under Dr. Hawkins's care, I learned a great deal about my own body and its problems. I discovered that I was both malnourished and highly allergic, and that I was strongly addicted to both caffeine and sugar. I was addicted to Serax, a tranquilizer which had been prescribed for my depression, and needed to be completely detoxified from both Serax and alcohol.

Dr. Hawkins and the staff at Brunswick House helped me to develop a program for a life without alcohol that would correct my addictions, relieve my allergies, and give me a sense of robust good health. I became involved in self-help groups that gave me insight into my life and disease. I realized that my father had been alcoholic and that his alcoholism had led to my parents' divorce and his premature death. I realized that my brother and I had spent much of our adult lives trying to prove that we were "stronger" than our father had been. This quest had killed my brother and almost killed me.

I got drunk for the first time when I was twelve years old. It was clear to me from the outset that I could drink a lot more than my friends, and I was pretty proud of that fact. I liked alcohol a lot, and when I was in college and graduate school I sometimes used a combination of uppers and downers to stay awake to study during exam periods. At no point in my life did it occur to me that my many accidents (including fights), failed relationships, medical problems, and depression were a consequence of my drinking. It was only after my alcoholism had been identified and treated that I was able to clearly see the path of carnage that alcoholism had cut through my life.

Since that summer of 1979, I have devoted my career to the field of alcoholism and its treatment. With the help of my staff, I have done an exhaustive search of the research literature on this disease in an effort to develop a truly comprehensive treatment program. I have attempted to integrate this knowledge into the treatment program at the facility where I am medical director, and have overseen the care of more than seventeen thousand patients with alcoholism. And I have performed an exhaustive study which documents the effectiveness of a bio-behavioral approach to this elusive and deadly disease.

There have been many mistakes made in the treatment of alcoholism over the years, and we have paid the price in the form of disease, death, and disability. It is time for us to take a new attitude toward alcoholism and to open our minds to the real nature of the disease. This book is an attempt to facilitate such a change and to dispel some of the dangerous myths which have impeded our efforts to fight alcoholism. If you or someone you love is suffering from alcoholism, it is my sincere hope that this book will help you avoid the pain and sorrow that alcoholism brought to my life and that it will help you find the health, contentment, and joy that I eventually found in my sobriety.

2

ALCOHOLISM— AN OVERVIEW

What is the nation's number one killer?

Cancer?

Heart disease?

Diabetes?

None of the above. In terms of lives lost, misery caused, productivity depleted, and simple dollars and cents, alcoholism leads the pack as the nation's number one killer. Consider[1]:

- Alcoholism is both a major cause and a contributor to the other killers of our time—most notably heart disease, stroke, liver disease, hypertension, and cancer.
- There were 10.5 million known alcoholics in the U.S. in 1985. An additional 7.2 million suffered from other negative effects of alcohol use.

- 18.3 million American adults are heavy drinkers (fourteen or more drinks per week). Of these, 12.1 million have one or more symptoms of alcoholism.
- One in every four American families has been afflicted by an alcohol-related problem.
- Alcohol abuse accounts for approximately ninety-eight thousand deaths annually, and this does not include the thousands of unrecognized alcohol-related deaths that occur each year.
- In 1983, alcoholism and alcohol abuse cost the nation $116.7 billion. And this number is rising; recent estimates place the yearly cost of alcoholism at over $200 billion.
- 60 percent of attempted suicides are alcoholics. Alcoholics make up 30 percent of successful suicides. The rising rate of teen suicide is almost certainly related to the rise in alcohol and drug use in this group.
- More than 60 percent of county jail inmates are incarcerated for alcohol-related crimes.
- Alcohol-related absenteeism and lost productivity cost U.S. industry in excess of forty-five billion dollars each year.
- More than 50 percent of fatal car accidents involve alcohol.
- Drinking is involved in an estimated 50 percent of spouse abuse cases and 38 percent of child abuse cases.
- Alcohol is implicated in 65 to 69 percent of all reported drownings.
- The mortality rate of alcoholics is *twice* that of the general population.

- Chronic brain injury caused by alcohol is second only to Alzheimer's disease as a known cause of mental deterioration in adults.

Not only is alcoholism the number one killer, but it is also taking its toll on progressively younger victims. While the federal government launches a war on drugs and urges children to "just say no" to crack:

- Alcohol is the number one drug of abuse among American youth. One in every three adolescents has experienced bad effects from alcohol use—from poor school performance to legal trouble.
- 36 percent of fourth-grade respondents to a *Weekly Reader* poll indicated that kids their age pushed them to drink beer, wine, or liquor.
- Alcohol-related highway deaths are the *number one* killer of fifteen- to twenty-four-year-olds, killing nearly nine thousand in 1986 alone.

Despite these facts, the federal government spends only three dollars on alcoholism research for every one hundred dollars spent on cancer research, and funding for alcohol treatment programs has been cut.

The recent legislation geared to fighting the war on drugs has virtually ignored alcohol as a drug of abuse, and actually resulted in decreases in funding for many cities and agencies.

The *known* costs of alcoholism exceed two hundred *billion* dollars each year. This price tag may be appalling, but it is actually only the tip of the iceberg.

It has been estimated that as many as 50 percent of the patients in the nation's hospitals have undiagnosed alcoholism as either the cause of or a contributing factor in their disease or injury. These patients are generally not included in the statistics on alcoholism.

Since alcoholism is both treatable and preventable it should be possible to cut the *total national health budget* by 20 percent—for a net savings of one hundred and ten *billion* dollars per year. The prevention, diagnosis, and treatment of alcoholism presents the most accessible way to cut our national health costs without compromising the quality of national health care. The possibilities are amazing.

How did we get into this predicament? How can thousands upon thousands of human beings die of this disease every year without any public outcry for better research and treatment?

Let's consider the way society looks at alcoholics. From biblical times onward, society has taken a dim view of alcoholics. The book of Deuteronomy advocates stoning drunkards, and the apostle Paul (in 1: Corinthians) classified drunkards with idolaters, swindlers, revilers, and other immoral persons.

Although drunkards were (and are) also viewed as comic characters (Shakespeare and Dean Martin have both made considerable use of drunk characters as comic relief), in the real world the most widely accepted "treatment" of alcoholism has been punishment—from public stoning to the "drunk tank." In fact, a study conducted in 1964 revealed that 62 percent of general hospitals refused to admit and treat alcoholic patients.[2]

This study was particularly alarming since it was conducted

eight years after the AMA house of delegates advocated the admission of patients with alcoholism to general hospitals.[3] The AMA's statement was a valiant attempt to bring alcoholism into the fold of medical practice, and suggested that educational programs and research on alcoholism be encouraged. In 1959, a proposed alcoholism curriculum was even sent to medical schools.[4] Unfortunately, seven years later, in 1966, nothing had been done with the proposed curriculum, and next to nothing had been done to encourage hospitals to (in the words of the AMA) deal with "the alcoholism problem."[5] When alcoholism finally was accepted as a disease, it was classified as a personality disorder, defined by the American Psychiatric Association as "alcohol dependence syndrome":

> a state, *psychic,* and *usually* also physical, resulting from taking alcohol, characterized by *behavioral* and other responses that always include a compulsion to take alcohol on a continuous or periodic basis *in order to experience its psychic effects* and *sometimes* to avoid the discomfort of its absence; *tolerance may or may not be present.* [emphasis added].[6]

As a result of this classification, alcoholism came to be viewed as a psychological disease, and the alcoholic's drinking behavior was considered a form of self-treatment for an underlying psychological problem. Treatment was geared toward resolving this problem through psychotherapy and support, and research was directed at finding the underlying personality characteristics that led to the abuse of alcohol. The myriad physical problems of alcoholics were considered side effects of the behavioral disorder.

In reality, the psychological theory of alcoholism isn't all that different from the moral one. According to the moralists, alcoholics drink because they are selfish, inconsiderate of others, and immoral. According to psychological theorists, alcoholics drink because they have a "premorbid personality" that makes them unable to deal with reality, face their responsibilities, or exercise self-control.

Both the psychological and the moral approach assume that alcoholics *choose* to drink and that the physical aspects of alcoholism are just side effects and wouldn't have occurred if the alcoholic had been strong (or smart or moral) enough to stop drinking. In both views, the responsibility (and/or the blame) for the alcoholic's condition rests with the alcoholic. As a result, the alcoholic is not viewed in the same sympathetic way we view the victims of other illnesses such as cancer.

This underlying belief has affected everything society, governments, insurers, and doctors have done about alcoholism. A huge industry has grown out of the psychological disease model of alcoholism. Alcoholism treatment expenditures are now estimated at fifteen billion dollars a year. Thousands of inpatient, outpatient, short-term, long-term, detoxification and/or rehabilitation clinics have sprung up across the nation. Employee assistance programs, private counseling clinics, and thousands of individual practitioners offer services to alcoholics—with the vast majority of these practitioners diligently trying to identify and treat the underlying psychological disorder that caused their patients' alcoholism.

Unfortunately, the vast majority fail to find that underlying cause, and large numbers of their patients never recover from alcoholism.

In 1985, an article in *Consumer's Research* estimated that out of every one hundred alcoholics, only forty are likely to get any treatment for their disease. Of these, twenty will leave treatment and die prematurely. Ten will manage to maintain sobriety for three to five years. Another ten will vacillate for several years. *Only five will achieve long-term measurable sobriety.* [7]

Despite the fact that treatment programs exist, thousands of alcoholics are closed out of treatment by unreasonable limitations on insurance coverage (limitations which the AMA recognized as unreasonable almost twenty-five years ago). It has been estimated that only 13 percent of the nation's alcoholics are in touch with treatment facilities and that only 9 percent of these were referred by a physicians. [8]

Even when treated, the alcoholic's future is far from secure. Numerous studies have shown that psychologically oriented treatment programs have little impact on the course of alcoholism. In fact, research has shown that treated alcoholics have the same mortality rate as those who are not treated. The following are just a few of the research findings on the effectiveness of alcoholism treatment:

- A study of an urban outpatient alcoholism program found that 45 percent of the patients were lost to follow-up within thirty days. [9]
- A 1975 review of 384 psychologically based treatment programs found that treatment had no significant impact on an alcoholic's chances of recovery. [10]
- A 1985 investigation of the status of alcoholics three years after treatment found that 85 percent were actively drinking. [11]

In recent years, studies have compared the effectiveness of inpatient versus outpatient treatment of alcoholism and found no difference in success rates between the two modes. Since outpatient treatment is cheaper, many insurers, employers, and policymakers have used these study findings as a justification for reductions in funding for inpatient treatment.

Why don't these other programs work? Why do 85 percent of alcoholics slip through the cracks and die of their disease? Because America's doctors, insurance companies, major corporations, politicians, and general public do not understand (or fully accept) the *real* nature of the disease of alcoholism.

These individuals and organizations are making decisions based on a view of alcoholism that is both outdated and unscientific. Decades of treatment programs have been based on a theory of alcoholism that virtually ignored the medical aspects of the disease. It is not surprising that their success rates have been low. The fact that they have had any success at all is amazing and a tribute to the dedication and perseverance of patients and counselors alike. But basing policy decisions on these results is like evaluating diabetes before the development of insulin. The prognosis for diabetic patients was grim, indeed, in the days before insulin. Now diabetes is a manageable disease. We are at a similar juncture with alcoholism. The powers that be that are cutting inpatient treatment funds fail to realize that inpatient and outpatient success rates are equally dismal because inpatient and outpatient treatment have been based on an incomplete model of alcoholism.

Alcoholism is the only *medical* disease which is routinely turned over to nonphysicians for management. Physicians are primarily involved with what are considered the medical side effects of alcoholism like liver disease or broken bones or pancreatitis.

So what? you may ask. Does it really matter who treats alcoholics, as long as they're treated? It certainly does. No rational person would send a diabetic to a psychologist for treatment, yet alcoholics, *who are suffering from a physical disease with widespread and chronic medical consequences,* are consistently referred to nonmedical persons for treatment when *they are still in severe medical distress.* No counselor, no matter how expert, can do an effective job if the person being treated is *unable to understand or make use of psychological counseling.*

In medicine, treatment should match the needs of the illness. If a medical problem is simple with a known cause and no complications (such as a simple fracture), treatment is equally simple. Diseases with more complex causes and effects (such as hypertension or diabetes) require more complex treatment with complete changes in life-style (from nutrition to exercise) as well as medication.

More than three decades of research on alcoholism has proven that alcoholism, like hypertension, is a very complex disease indeed.

Do you remember when you took your first drink? Was it a can of beer in the backseat of a car? Was it some spiked punch at a sweet sixteen party? Was it a swig of cheap wine or brandy at a winter high school football game? Was it a glass of champagne at a cousin's wedding?

Each year hundreds of thousands of American teenagers go through the rite of passage of the first drink. The majority of these individuals will live out their lives as social drinkers. Some will become problem drinkers who abuse alcohol and use it as an escape or who drink far too much on social occasions. Only about 10 percent of individuals who drink will become alcoholics.

Alcoholism, unlike drug addiction, is *selective. All* human beings, if exposed to heroin, cocaine, Valium, crack, etc., will become addicted after sufficient time. But it takes a unique biochemistry to make someone an alcoholic. Individuals with this unique body chemistry are carrying a biological time bomb—and once the bomb is detonated, there is no turning back. They have entered a statistical category that virtually guarantees them premature death from accident, suicide, stroke, liver failure, cardiovascular complications, and a dozen other causes, not to mention disfigurement, brain damage, imprisonment, and the destruction of all close relationships.

These people continue to drink, and to increase the amount they drink, because they have no choice.

They have become alcoholic because of:

A. *genetic predisposition* manifested as an inability to properly metabolize alcohol, which leads to
B. *tolerance* and *addiction* to alcohol as the body alters its normal metabolism, resulting in a syndrome of
C. *malnutrition* and *toxicity* so severe that any attempt to stop drinking causes
D. painful *physical withdrawal,* whose most severe manifestations—delirium tremens—can be fatal; in fact, as many as 20 percent of alcoholics who get D.T.'s die.

A-B-C-D. A simple, ugly progression of a complex and deadly disease. This progression may vary in time and severity, depending on the individual's physical makeup but it occurs in *every* alcoholic. And it is why alcoholics can't "just stop drinking." The biochemistry of the alcoholic has been so radically altered and is so dependent on the presence of alcohol that stopping drinking cold turkey could be fatal.

The progression of alcoholism results in a syndrome of:

- malnutrition
- organ damage
- systemic toxicity
- neurochemical imbalances
- immunological disorders
- neurological and endocrine malfunctions

so severe that normal metabolism, diet, and behavior are virtually impossible for the alcoholic patient. This picture is considerably more complicated than the simple "premorbid personality" with "some medical side effects" that most alcoholism treatment programs believe they are dealing with.

Most treatment programs either ignore or grossly underestimate the medical consequences of alcoholism. Twenty-eight days (the usual inpatient stay) of abstinence, group therapy, and counseling will not alleviate chronic malnutrition, restore normal brain function, reverse toxic effects, or teach the alcoholic the skills needed to maintain a comfortable alcohol-free life outside the hospital. These things require time and a comprehensive treatment program that addresses the unique medical needs of the alcoholic.

It is time to adopt a new view of alcoholism—one which acknowledges the true biochemical complexity of this disease and approaches treatment from a rational medical perspective. Restoration of the disordered biochemical state of the alcoholic is the only reasonable foundation for treatment. Any attempt at psychotherapy prior to such restoration is like trying to psychoanalyze a patient who has just been struck on the head with a brick.

It is this misconception of the nature of alcoholism that is responsible for the dismal results of so many well-intentioned treatment programs. Alcoholism is not an untreatable disease, and alcoholics are not hopeless patients. But treatment must have a strong biomedical foundation if it is to succeed. Treatment without such a foundation is like a house built on sand.

My colleagues and I arrived at this conclusion after an exhaustive review of the research on the biological and genetic nature of alcoholism, and a careful evaluation of the studies which have made use of these concepts in the treatment of alcoholism.

One such study, performed by Ruth Guenther in 1982,[12] made use of nutritional education, therapy, and vitamin supplementation with exceptionally good results. Of the patients who were involved in the nutritional program, more than 60 percent were sober at the end of six months. Of the matched control group who had not received such nutritional care, more than 80 percent were actively drinking.

Guenther and her colleagues focused on nutrition in their study. My colleagues and I decided to develop and evaluate a more comprehensive treatment program that would address not only the nutritional but metabolic, immunological, neurochemical, psychological, and behavioral aspects of alcoholism.[13]

Our study was conducted with a group of 111 alcoholics who were treated at the alcoholism hospital where I serve as medical director. Their ages ranged from twenty-two to sixty-six, and all had long and dismal histories of alcohol abuse. Thirty-eight percent of the study participants were addicted to other drugs besides alcohol (marijuana, cocaine, and tranquilizers—particularly Valium—were the leaders). Fully 78 percent of these individuals had received some sort of alcoholism treatment at least once before.

Comprehensive diagnosis and evaluation of these patients revealed that most of them were in advanced stages of the disease with extensive malnutrition, food sensitivities, and physical pathology. Nearly half of them were suffering from liver disease. More than 40 percent of these patients had significant problems in metabolizing glucose, and 98 percent had adverse reactions to foods—particularly grains and other ingredients found in alcoholic beverages. On the whole, these patients' physical states and histories did not bode well for successful treatment.

While in the hospital, each patient was put on a dietary program that provided necessary nutrients while rotating or eliminating foods that produced adverse reactions and limited chemical additives, preservatives, and highly refined foods. (For a more detailed explanation of such a nutritional program, see chapter 16.) We put considerable emphasis on education about the medical nature of alcoholism and on learning a new life-style that would promote a feeling of constant health and well-being. Workshops, role-playing, Alcoholics Anonymous

(AA) meetings, and individual counseling were an integral part of the program, and we stressed the importance of maintaining a healthy life-style when outside the hospital.

Upon release, these patients remained involved in a program of follow-up care, monitoring, and education for twelve months. They continued the nutritional program, counseling, and AA involvement and came into our office for monthly follow-up visits and medical evaluation. Their drinking status was monitored through random urine tests and regular blood tests as well as personal interviews with loved ones and employers (if the employer knew of the subject's alcoholism).

We found that the first few months after inpatient treatment were usually the hardest. In several cases we had to take very active measures to stay in contact with patients—from calling repeatedly to actually going to their homes to find out what was going on. It was necessary to provide lots of support and encouragement as these men and women took the first steps to adjusting to life outside the hospital without alcohol.

At the end of twelve months, we were still in regular contact with ninety (81 percent) of the original 111 patients. Three of the lost twenty-one had been excluded from the study because they had moved away, and one was still in treatment but was not being considered because his primary addiction was to cocaine, not alcohol. The remaining seventeen patients had evaded our efforts at staying in contact.

Of the patients who were treated for all twelve months, 74 percent were sober and physically well at their twelve-month dates. In fact, 67 percent of the sober and stable patients had been totally abstinent without complications for the entire time. Several patients slipped during the early part of their recovery, found that the experience convinced them that they could never drink again, and remained abstinent from then on. Only fifteen of the sixty-seven sober and stable patients had more than one slip during their first twelve months of recovery.

These results prove that it is indeed possible to treat alcoholics successfully—but the treatment must be both comprehensive and long-term if it is to have the most effect. Many of these patients had a difficult time in the early days of recovery and might have returned to drinking without the care and support they received from our staff and their families. As their physical status improved, however, these patients reported feeling less and less of a need for alcohol and more and more of a sense of confidence and general well-being. The results of their physical and lab tests confirmed their continued progress.

These findings, and the rapidly growing body of knowledge on the effects of alcohol addiction, hold out the greatest hope for persons with alcoholism. It is my firm belief that alcoholism treatment can have success rates in excess of 80 percent if treatment is properly designed, coordinated, and followed up. But until this knowledge is more widely distributed and integrated into existing treatment programs, it is up to you—the loved ones of the alcoholic—to become familiar with the reality of the disease and learn what to look for in a good treatment plan.

3
ALTERNATIVE "HIGHS"— THE NATURAL WAY

At a recent class in the treatment facility where I serve as medical director, I asked a group of recovering alcoholics what they felt alcohol and drugs had done for them. Their answers were illuminating.

"It emptied my bank account."
"It gave me chronic heartburn and diarrhea."
"It destroyed my self-esteem."
"It made me feel like a dollar ninety-eight."
"It made me horny, then I couldn't get it up."
"It made me the life of a lot of parties that I couldn't remember the next day."
"It got me a divorce."
"It lost me my job."
"It ruined my teeth."
"It ruined my liver."
"It ruined my life."

None of these men and women had actively set out to achieve these states of misery. All of them thought that alcohol was fun, something to be enjoyed and indulged in at will. After all, it's legal.

Alcoholics, Valium addicts, heroin users, cocaine addicts, chocaholics, etc., etc., ad infinitum, are the tragic by-products of our national obsession with immediate gratification, quick cures, and "getting high." If we can't sleep, we take a pill. If we're overweight, we look for appetite suppressants and miracle drugs that will "melt" body fat. If we can't get up in the morning, we drink several cups of coffee. And if we really want to enjoy ourselves socially, we drink.

Some of the best minds in advertising make a very nice living encouraging these beliefs. In 1987, for example, the alcohol industry spent 1.3 billion dollars on advertising, 809.1 million of it on television spots for beer (620 million dollars), wine (76.4 million dollars), and various types of coolers (111 million dollars), while 1.7 million dollars went into advertisements for distilled liquors on cable channels.[1] These skillfully wrought advertisements tell us in clear and graphic terms that the way to social acceptance, sex, athletic prowess, and all-around good times is through alcohol. Thousands more commercial advertisements exhort us to take any one of hundreds of pills, tablets, capsules, or caplets to relieve our aches, pains, sleepiness, sleeplessness, or overweight.

In between these calls to drugs or liquor we see thousands of commercials for a variety of "foods" and candies that have all the nutritional value of Styrofoam (maybe less). Children are encouraged to eat chocolate-coated-marshmallow-filled-real-fruit-flavored-sugar-bombs cereal as "part of a balanced breakfast." (What, one wonders, is the other part—potato chips?) Various candy bars are recommended as quick pick-me-ups with audacious advertising campaigns that claim they are nutritious because they contain peanut butter or minuscule amounts of granola. Is it any wonder that alcoholics are malnourished when they live in a world which promotes a diet of almost complete garbage and a life-style of instant cures and quick fixes?

Of course, if more people understood what these quick fixes really do, we'd have a lot fewer drug addicts and alcoholics in this country. But most of us don't find out the real price of these instant highs until the bill arrives.

Incipient alcoholics don't go out on Saturday night and say "Hey, let's destroy our livers, impair our brain metabolisms, give ourselves early osteoporosis, cancer, hypertension, and heart disease, and increase our chances of driving the car off a cliff!" Cocaine addicts don't start out saying, "Any drug that makes you paranoid *and* impotent is the drug for me!" Smokers don't light up thinking, "Oh boy, I can't wait for my lungs to fill up with tar and start melting from emphysema!" And children don't eat several bowls of sugar-coated cereal with cries of "Oh, goodie, now I can be hyperactive and incoherent for the rest of the day!"

At this time, most of the population of the United States has been rendered toxic and malnourished in the interest of short-term economic gain.[2] And we have simultaneously been brainwashed into believing that this life-style of junk food and quick fixes is the American way of life and that we've never had it so good. We really believe that refined sugar, refined carbohydrates, caffeine, saturated and hydrogenated fats, and foods processed to the point of unrecognizability are the American way to eat. Add nine pounds of chemical additives a year, stir in air and water polution, mix with toxic chemicals in the work and home, and you have a quick and easy recipe for disaster. When alcohol and drugs are added to this formula, our already strained metabolisms simply give up.

The vast majority of Americans have no more understanding of addiction and nutrition than they do of how to build a thermonuclear device. They rely on advertising—three quarters of which comes from drug, alcohol, and food companies—for all their information. And what appallingly inaccurate information it is.

Consider, for example, the lowly loaf of white bread, made with "enriched wheat flour." Wheat is a marvelous grain, and in its complete state contains all but four of the essential nutrients. When it is refined into white flour, however, the resulting white powder is good for making paste, but little else. Refining away the wheat germ and bran strips away as much as 80 percent of wheat's nutrient value, and adds 7 percent to its calories.

"Enrichment" restores only a handful of the more than twenty-five nutrients lost during refining (including 85 percent of the fiber). The net result is a food that won't keep a lab rat alive for ninety days, much less a human.[3] One critic of the modern food industry compared enrichment to a mugging. If the mugger pointed a gun at you and told you to strip nude, turn over all your clothes, jewelry, money, credit cards, wallet, and shoes, and then thought better of it and returned your coat, socks, and enough cash to get home you *might* feel enriched (although it's doubtful). White flour, processed cheese foods, and most instant food products are the nutritional equivalent of a mugging.

The overwhelming message being directed at the American people is that if it is fast, easy, and a guaranteed instant high it has to be good. The way to keep yourself alert and satisfied is to have a candy bar. You can "keep them home for breakfast" by feeding them cakes first thing in the morning. Soft drinks will make you smile and feel more lively. Any illness, from a head cold to hemorrhoids, can be cured with the help of your friendly neighborhood drugstore. And beer, wine, and liquor will make you sexier, more popular, more athletic, and more fun at parties.

When, after years of improperly feeding and caring for our bodies, we find ourselves feeling fatigued and unwell, we go to the doctor. And the doctor, as much product of the system as we are, will usually not look too deeply into our nutritional and metabolic status, decide we are "stressed" and prescribe a "minor tranquilizer," such as Valium.

To counter this flow of destructive drivel we have public service announcements on TV and radio telling us to "just say no" or trying to scare us with descriptions of the horrors of drug abuse and the dangers of malnutrition. Of course, these messages are usually surrounded by beer, cereal, and candy commercials which are much better produced and far more compelling. The 200 million dollars the alcoholic beverage industry spent to combat alcohol abuse and drunk driving comes up pitifully short when compared to its 1.3 billion dollar advertising budget and the 175 million that was spent on promotional campaigns.[4]

The great flaw in most public service announcements is that

they focus almost entirely on *not* doing something. Don't drink. Don't do drugs. Don't beat your children. Don't gamble. While these messages are all perfectly valid, they don't answer the equally valid question, *What should I do instead?*

If you believe most of the nation's advertisers, the answer would be "nothing." Life without some sort of drug, alcohol, or junk food is like no life at all. Fortunately for us all, the exact opposite is true.

Anything drugs can do, the brain can do better. For every smartly packaged over-the-counter or prescription drug, for every chic recreational drug, for every substance we gulp down to feel well enough to make it through the day, there is a better, natural equivalent produced within our own bodies. The human brain produces far more powerful drugs than any laboratory, and it does it for free.

It was once thought that the cells of the brain (neurons) were rather like the electrical system in a house or car, and communicated through electrical impulses. In reality, the cells of the brain are not even physically connected, and communication between neurons is a complex electro*chemical* process.

Neurons are separated by a gap called the synapse. They produce specific chemicals called neurotransmitters which filter across this gap and stimulate receptor sites on neighboring neural cells. This stimulation causes an electrical charge within the cell and also results in the production and release of more neurotransmitter. Simply put, it is an electrochemical domino effect.

This system even has a built-in recycling plant in the form of a reuptake mechanism which removes excess neurotransmitter from the synapse and processes it for later use.

The brain's neurotransmitters are highly specialized, with specific functions and effects. They regulate everything from when we feel hungry to how we respond to chance encounters with large bears in the woods. One group of neurotransmitters (the endorphins and enkephalins among them) are responsible for the suppression of pain that we experience in times of crisis—for example, making it possible for a football player to be able to keep playing after hurting a knee. In fact, when these neurotransmitters are assayed, we find they are far more powerful than painkillers produced in a lab.

It is important to understand the neurotransmitters if you are to understand the effects of alcohol, drugs, and even certain foods. These substances are popular because they are capable of affecting—directly or indirectly—the balance of neurotransmitters in the brain. They can do this in a variety of ways: by being structurally similar to natural neurotransmitters and stimulating receptor sites; by interfering with reuptake so that more of the neurotransmitter stays in the synapse and increases stimulation; and by combining with other biochemicals to form substances which can either block reuptake or stimulate receptors (and sometimes both). No drug will work unless it is interacting with or mimicking a chemical that is already produced by the brain.

Why then aren't we high all the time?

Primarily, because our bodies are considerably smarter than our conscious minds.

A basic rule of physics is that for every action there is an equal and opposite reaction. When you've experienced the adrenaline rush of getting away from a bear in the woods, the natural follow-up is a need to rest and recuperate. The body instinctively keeps things in balance. It is when this balance gets disrupted that we run into trouble.

Every time you drink a cup of coffee, smoke a cigarette, have a drink, eat a candy bar, or do a line of cocaine you are disrupting your body's natural balance—replacing natural chemicals with unnatural ones. You may get a quick and gratifying response, but the downside will be correspondingly quick and a lot less gratifying. In fact, in many cases, the downside is actually worse than the predrugged state. You go down further than you went up, and afterward require more of the drug to get the desired effect.

The popularity of most drugs is a consequence of the speed and intensity of their effects. Eating a radish will eventually have an effect on your brain, but radishes don't sell for two thousand dollars a kilogram on the street. Cocaine is derived from a plant, but its effect on the brain is immediate and a lot more dramatic and enjoyable (for a little while) than eating a radish. (In chapter 15 I will go into greater detail about how each of the various classes of drugs affect the neurochemical balance of the brain.)

In general, the brain responds to the presence of exogenous (outside the body) chemicals by altering its production of endogenous (natural) neurochemicals. For example, the brain responds to repeated doses of heroin by cutting down on its production of the various types of endorphins. When a heroin user stops taking heroin, it takes the brain a while to resume normal production of endorphins. As a result, the abstinent heroin user suffers from a *deficiency* of endorphins, and this causes a variety of highly unpleasant symptoms. Alcohol, as we shall see, has a much wider physiological and neurochemical impact than heroin and impairs a lot more than endorphin production.

To oversimplify a bit, your brain responds to outside chemical influences by going on a sort of sit-down strike. It interprets the presence of these extra chemicals as an excess of natural neurotransmitters and slows down or alters its production accordingly. Since many of the most popular recreational drugs also affect reuptake, drug use also reduces the amount of raw material that the cells of the brain have to produce neurotransmitters. When the exogenous substances are removed, the brain isn't able to resume normal production quickly enough to make up the deficit. As a result you feel lousy, and so have another drink, pill, or cup of coffee, thus starting the cycle all over again. In the long run, you become entirely dependent on the unnatural chemicals—from caffeine and corn syrup to alcohol, cocaine, or Valium.

To be fair, none of these dire consequences are inevitable. Most of these substances are not really dangerous if they are used in moderation. For centuries, a wide variety of drugs have been used ceremonially in many cultures. But these ceremonies were rare events, not daily activities, and the drugs themselves were usually in their natural form—as plants or plant derivatives.

The substances which we are ingesting on a daily basis are highly refined and far more potent than their original plant forms. And laboratory produced drugs are specifically designed to be as potent as possible. We've come a long way from the ceremonial peace pipe or peyote ritual.

Not only have we forgotten how to do things in moderation, but also we have almost entirely forgotten how to *trust our own bodies.* In our frantic search for the magic food, pill, or drink that will make our lives more enjoyable, we have lost sight of the fact that *good health is the greatest high,* and it doesn't come in a bottle.

It is possible to naturally alter the body's homeostasis, and increase the normal levels of the endorphins, enkephalins, serotonin, and other neurochemicals. It is possible to feel well, energetic, sexy, and joyful without the help of a drink or a pill. It is possible to get up in the morning and go to bed at night without the help of caffeine and sleeping pills. And all it really takes is a change in attitude about your own health and some educated choices about your life-style.

Simply making the choice isn't enough, of course. It takes time and commitment. The body is a remarkable organism, capable of adjusting to almost any situation, but it cannot rehabilitate itself automatically. If you have done any gardening you know that a plant that has been negelected and has withered away to the verge of death requires tender care and feeding to be brought back to blooming health. Your body is far more complicated than a plant and deserves at least as much consideration and care.

Don't be fooled into handing your life over to the liquor, tobacco, and food companies who are interested in profits, not your health. No distillery is going to tell you what alcohol can do to your body. No cereal company is going to admit that their boxes have more nutritional value than their cereals. And no drug company is going to tell you that your illness can be cured just as easily with rest and good nutrition as with their pill.

You carry the potential for a long and healthy life within every cell of your body—the potential for a consistent, natural high that won't disappear when the alcohol clears from your system. In order to realize this potential you must learn the basics of how to live a truly healthy life. This book can be a valuable guide on the road to such a life, since alcoholism may be the most dramatic example of an unhealthy life-style. The road back from alcoholism is also the road to good health for those without alcoholism. The principles of nutrition, exercise, and behavior which I outline in chapters 12 and 14 apply to everyone, not just alcoholics, and should be applied to the entire family, not just the family member with alcoholism.

Before we can begin to discuss the process of recovering from alcoholism, however, we must understand the way alcoholism develops—the A-B-C-D progression I outlined earlier. Let us take them one at a time.

4
GENETICS

Alcoholism runs in families. In a recent study at our clinic on Long Island, we found that 89 percent of our patients had at least one blood relative with alcoholism, and over half had alcoholic parents.[1] But for most of history the reason for this phenomenon has remained elusive.

Psychological theorists long assumed that alcoholism was a form of learned behavior—if you grow up in an alcoholic household, you learn to be alcoholic. (Unless, of course, you learn to *avoid* alcohol completely!)

But what if one of your parents was alcoholic and you were raised apart from them? What if you were adopted?

These questions have intrigued many researchers, and over the years a wide variety of scientists have performed extensive studies on the children of alcoholics to determine whether genetics, rather than environment (nature versus nurture), is the crucial factor in the development of alcoholism.

To date, more than a hundred scientific studies have indicated that something genetic is indeed at work in alcoholism, and the pool of evidence is growing. Children of alcoholics are at four times greater risk of developing alcoholism than those of nonalcoholics—regardless of whether or not they were raised by their alcoholic parent.[2] And comparisons of the incidence of alcoholism in identical twins who had been separated at birth—one raised in the household with an alcoholic parent and one raised in a nonalcoholic household—found that there was no significant difference in the incidences of alcoholism between the two groups. In other words, environment didn't have any real effect on whether or not these identical twins developed alcoholism. However, identical twins *are* both more likely to develop alcoholism than fraternal (nonidentical) twins. Fifty-eight percent of identical twin children of alcoholics both developed alcoholism (even when they were raised apart), while only 28 percent of fraternal twins both developed alcoholism.[3]

Simply put, the closer you are, genetically, to an alcoholic, the more likely you are to develop the disease yourself. The children (and grandchildren) of alcoholics appear to have inherited a unique biological response to alcohol. Not a moral weakness, not a personality flaw, but a genetically encoded difference in the way they metabolize alcohol. And this genetic predisposition holds true no matter where, how, or with whom they are raised.

If you are the child of an alcoholic and were separated from your natural parents at birth, *you are still at high risk* of becoming an alcoholic if you drink. If you were raised by people who were devout fundamentalists and believed that alcohol is the tool of Satan, you are still at high risk.

This high risk is not, however, related to a psychological disorder. Donald Goodwin investigated the possibility that alcoholism was actually a symptom of some other psychological problem by comparing the histories of two groups of adoptees: one group with alcoholic natural parents and one without. Detailed analyses of the social and psychological histories of these two groups revealed that the only significant difference between them was the rate of alcoholism. The children of alcoholics were not more prone to any psychiatric disorders.[4]

Of course, the mere fact that the children of alcoholics are more likely to become alcoholics themselves does not explain how this occurs. What is it, exactly, that makes these people different from everyone else who drinks?

A clue to this mystery can be found in a very unlikely place—the People's Republic of China. The Chinese, who have one of the most ancient and glorious traditions in the preparation of meals, as well as one of the world's most varied and complex cuisines, use dramatically less alcohol in all its forms than Americans and Europeans. The social world of the Chinese revolves around the teahouse or the noodle house rather than pubs or bars.

This apparent lack of interest in alcohol is not only cultural but also biological. Approximately 60 percent of Chinese (and many other Orientals) have negative responses to even small doses of alcohol. These responses can range from mild flushing over the body, face, and earlobes to headaches, dizziness, severe drops in blood pressure, rapid heart beat, tingling, and even hives. Some individuals become so violently ill after drinking alcohol that they will be incapacitated for as much as twenty-four hours.[5]

In effect, many Chinese have an inborn physiological aversion to alcohol. Drinking alcoholic beverages is not enjoyable for these individuals because of the way in which their bodies process alcohol. This difference in alcohol metabolism is a result of genetically determined enzyme activity.

Enzymes are crucial to the normal function of the human body. They are the proteins which make the chemical reactions of metabolism possible by catalyzing or accelerating biochemical reactions. It is the enzymes in yeast which cause wine to ferment, and the enzyme rennin is used to make cheese.

In the body, enzymes serve very specific functions in the breakdown of various products, including nutrients. The absence or malfunction of a specific enzyme can have widespread and sometimes fatal effects throughout the body. Enzyme variations are common throughout humanity, and many are quite benign. At present there are more than two hundred known inborn differences in metabolism that occur in human beings.

One of the most dramatic examples of a potentially deadly inborn difference in metabolism is phenylketonuria or PKU. In PKU there is a deficiency of phenylalanine hydroxylase, which breaks down phenylalanine—an amino acid found in most proteins, including milk. Newborns with PKU cannot process phenylalanine, and toxic levels build up causing extensive central nervous system damage. If PKU goes undetected it can result in epilepsy, seizures, and severe mental retardation.

Fortunately, a simple test can detect parents who are carriers of the PKU gene, as well as identifying newborns with the disease. With proper dietary restrictions, the potentially disastrous effects of PKU can be avoided, and the children grow up normally.

PKU is a good example of a case where the *risk* of disease or damage (in this case mental retardation) is inherited, not the disease itself. As long as phenylketonurics avoid phenylalanine, their health will remain stable. Similarly, many Chinese avoid alcohol to avoid the negative effects produced by their unique biochemistry.

At the other end of the biochemical spectrum from the Chinese, we find the alcoholic. The alcoholic, too, has a unique enzymatic response to alcohol. But the experience of the alcoholic is *positive,* not negative. Unlike the Chinese, who may feel markedly ill after taking alcohol, or the average Caucasian, who feels relaxed and at ease after a drink or two but begins to lose motor control and coherence after a few more, the potential alcoholic actually exhibits improved hand-eye coordination and muscular control after drinking.

This rather startling finding is one of many being discovered by the rapidly growing field of research on the biochemical and neurological effects of alcohol on the children of alcoholics. It is now clear that the children of alcoholics actually respond differently to alcohol than their peers, and these responses begin with their very first drink.

In comparison with matched control subjects, the sons of alcoholics respond to alcohol with:

- less feelings of drunkenness
- improved hand-eye coordination
- improved muscle control
- lowered hormonal responses (less of a stress reaction)[6]

Sons of alcoholics (even those who have never drunk before) also have different patterns of brain wave activity, both before and after drinking,[7] and some researchers have noted higher serum (blood) levels of acetaldehyde in these subjects after drinking than in the sons of nonalcoholic control subjects.[8]

As we shall see in the next chapter, acetaldehyde is a crucial part of the biology of alcoholism, and the difference in acetaldehyde metabolism may be one of the enzymatic links to the genetics of this disease.

From a behavioral perspective, these findings mean that the potential alcoholic is receiving very different biological messages in response to alcohol than other persons. In effect, the message is: Alcohol is good, it makes you feel better, you can perform tasks more easily, it is your friend. This message is deceptive, however, because each drink is also slowly altering the potential alcoholic's biochemistry, making it more and more difficult to do without alcohol.

There may come a time when the genetic susceptibility to alcoholism, like PKU, will be able to be detected *before* the disease develops. It is my belief that, with proper funding, such a screen could be developed within the next three years and allow us to detect at-risk individuals before they drink.

Until that time, however, the alcoholic must understand that this biological trap was sprung a long time ago, and that escaping from it requires medical help. It cannot be escaped alone. The alcoholic cannot just stop drinking through the exercise of will. In the world of alcoholism, metabolism is stronger than free will.

5

TOLERANCE AND ADDICTION

Because the at-risk person gets such reinforcing effects from alcohol, he or she is more likely to drink on a regular basis and in large amounts. Friends may marvel at and even admire this person's good head for liquor, but this tolerance masks serious and potentially deadly biological changes.

Alcohol is a poison. Whenever you drink, your liver responds by breaking the alcohol down and eliminating it as quickly as possible. First, the liver breaks alcohol down into hydrogen and acetaldehyde. Acetaldehyde—a chemical relative of formaldehyde—is also toxic and is further oxidized into acetic acid. Acetic acid is then broken down into oxygen and water and excreted.

When the liver is consistently flooded with alcohol, however, it responds with certain metabolic adaptations to cope with the increased demand. The threshold point at which this adaptation actually occurs can vary considerably—and may even be genetically determined—but the result is the same.

The liver adapts by establishing an additional system for processing alcohol—the microsomal ethanol oxidizing system, or MEOS.[1] The MEOS increases the ability of the liver to process alcohol and also increases its production of acetaldehyde.

On the surface, this seems like an ideal arrangement. The MEOS allows the liver to break down alcohol faster than before. But the MEOS does *not* speed up the elimination of acetaldehyde. In fact, this highly toxic by-product of alcohol remains in the system, where it kills off the liver cells that would normally break it down, and chemically binds to various proteins.

The MEOS is actually a sort of biochemical catch-22. Because their livers can process more alcohol than before, these individuals can drink more with less obvious effects. This phenomenon is called tolerance.

However, the MEOS also *requires* considerably more alcohol to maintain its functioning than the normal alcohol processing system. This leads to an increased biological *need* for alcohol in order to maintain the new order. The body thus becomes addicted to alcohol in order to function. And the amount of alcohol required to feel normal increases as tolerance increases. Meanwhile, acetaldehyde is accumulating, causing cellular damage and adaptations in other systems, particularly in the brain.

Acetaldehyde is a remarkably "friendly" chemical. As we shall see in the next chapter, it binds easily with many other compounds, including the neurochemicals called the endogenous catecholamines. Researchers have found that when acetaldehyde combines with these neurochemicals, the resulting compounds—tetrahydroisoquinolines (TIQs) and salsolinol—

are sufficiently similar to the body's naturally occurring opiates—the endorphins—to fool the receptors designed for these neurochemicals.[2] It is thought that when TIQs and salsolinol occupy the spaces meant for the endorphins, the body interprets this as an indication that there is a sufficient supply of endorphins.

Functionally, this means that the alcohol addict may be experiencing a process very similar to heroin addiction. The presence of man-made chemicals in the brain causes the brain to slow down or stop production of naturally occurring neurochemicals.[3] When the artificial supply is taken away, the brain is not able to compensate fast enough, and the addict experiences depression, anxiety, and the various psychological symptoms of withdrawal. In the alcoholic, there is widespread disruption of the production of many of the neurochemicals which regulate emotions and moods, as well as those which regulate appetite, sleep, sexual drive, and every other regulatory function of the brain.[4] In effect, alcoholism takes control of every aspect of the alcoholic's life until everything he or she does is dependent on feeding the addiction. The cycle of tolerance and addiction is progressive. Although the alcoholic may not show signs of drunkenness or odd behavior until well into the disease, his or her body will demand more and more alcohol in order to function, until he or she will need to take alcohol throughout the day, often starting early in the morning. There is no maintenance dose for alcohol; it is an unrelenting master that makes increasing demands over time. It is only when the tolerance–addiction cycle has been stretched to the limit and the cells and organs and systems have reached a very high degree of malnourishment and toxicity that public drunkenness becomes the norm for the alcoholic. I have often been amazed at the number of wives, sons, daughters, husbands, and friends of alcoholics who have told me, "But I've never seen him (or her) drunk!" without realizing what a telltale sign heavy drinking without drunkenness is. The drunks that you have seen on the stage and screen are not representations of the reality of alcoholism. The "Hollywood drunk" stumbling around the street, propping up lampposts, being thrown out of bars for talking to pink elephants is a myth. The skid row figures that most people associate with alcoholism are only the farthest (and most tragic) end of the spectrum. Most alcoholics look no different from the person who looks back at you from the mirror each morning.

6

MALNUTRITION AND TOXICITY

If you are like most Americans, the word "malnutrition" brings to mind tragic images of spindly limbed children with distended bellies and sad eyes. Malnutrition is something that happens in the Third World during droughts, famines, or war.

What most of us do not realize is that these dramatic signs of starvation are only one small aspect of the broad spectrum of malnutrition. Malnutrition is more than just the absence of food; it is the absence of *nutrients* in the right amounts and correct balance.

The absence of even a single nutrient can have very serious physical and mental consequences. One of the most striking examples of such a deficiency disease is pellagra, caused by a deficiency of vitamin B_3 (niacin).

Pellagra is characterized by the "four Ds": dermatitis (rashes and skin lesions), diarrhea, dementia, and death. The third *D*—dementia—was responsible for the institutionalization of thousands of people in the rural South in the twenties. Corn, the dietary staple of this region (along with fatback pork and molasses, contains a form of niacin which cannot be absorbed by the intestinal tract unless it has been treated with an alkali (as in the making of tortillas). Corn is also deficient in trypto-phan, which helps the body synthesize niacin. As a result, these seemingly well-fed people were massively deficient in niacin.

When better nutrition was instituted in the mental hospitals of the South, the inpatient population dropped remarkably. It was not until 1937, when niacin was isolated and identified, that the specific relationship between pellagra and niacin defi-ciency was understood. Only then did physicians realize that a single nutrient—niacin—was at the root of most of the psychiatric problems in these patients.

Pellagra is just one example of the havoc that can be caused by the lack of a single vitamin. Yet the subtleties of malnutri-tion are lost on many medical practitioners, particularly when dealing with alcoholic patients. Few doctors recognize the malnutrition and widespread cellular poisoning that are the true root of the bizarre behavior of alcoholics.

The alcoholic consumes 50 percent or more of his or her total calories in the form of alcohol. Imagine, for a moment, what it would be like to cut your usual meal in half and replace it with a slow poison. That, in essence, is what the alcoholic is doing. Moreover, the remaining calories are almost always in the form of junk foods—pretzels, doughnuts, sweets, and other quick-energy sources. The alcoholic is consuming calories, it's true, but they are nutritionally useless, empty calories which actually *deplete* the body's stores of essential nutrients. With each drink and each junk food meal, the alcoholic is forging another link in a chain of malnutrition and toxicity that is progressively destroying his or her body.[1] The specific links in this chain are as follows.

Appetite. Alcohol can cross the blood/brain barrier which prevents most substances from directly affecting the cells of the brain, and has toxic effects on many brain regions. It particularly affects the cells of the midbrain that regulate the sensations of appetite. As a result, alcohol suppresses the alcoholic's desire for food, even while it encourages alcohol intake.

Energy. Alcohol liberates a lot of energy (7.1 calories per gram) without providing essential nutrients. Thus, the energy provided by alcohol is short-lived and there are no backup stores of nutrients to be drawn on. This shortage of long-term energy sources is related to the next link in the chain.

Glucose. After the initial rush of energy provided by alcohol, most alcoholics experience a correspondingly severe down swing due to the abrupt drop in blood glucose levels (hypoglycemia).[2] Most alcoholics treat the fatigue, depression, and loss of energy of hypoglycemia by eating foods high in sugar or other refined carbohydrates, by drinking caffeinated beverages, or smoking (nicotine is a stimulant). These "cures" are equally short-lived, however, and the cycle inevitably repeats itself, causing widespread disruption of normal carbohydrate metabolism.

This cycle of abrupt rises and drops in blood sugar is both contributed to and encouraged by the brain's adaptation to alcohol. Because alcohol crosses the blood/brain barrier with such ease, the brain adapts to the presence of alcohol by learning to use it as a fuel instead of glucose. This neurochemical shift alters and impairs the body's ability to burn glucose and encourages abnormal peaks and valleys in circulating glucose levels. As we shall see later, these peaks and valleys have very important behavioral and psychological ramifications.

Malabsorption. Alcohol is a poison, and its effects on the tissues of the digestive tract are enormously destructive. Alcohol irritates the linings of the stomach, intestinal tract, and colon to such a degree that these tissues become more permeable—allowing partially digested food proteins to pass into the bloodstream, where they provoke abnormal immune responses. In addition, alcohol causes drastic shifts in content and volume of many gastric secretions, causing further tissue damage and painful physical symptoms.[3]

Utilization. Alcohol severely damages the organs that are responsible for processing, utilizing, and distributing nutrients—particularly the liver and pancreas. By drastically altering the biochemical processes in these organs, alcohol causes widespread impairments in the metabolism of amino acids, lipids, vitamins, minerals, and glucose. As a result of these changes, the few nutrients that the alcoholic does take in are not utilized or stored effectively.[4]

Excretion. Alcohol not only interferes with absorption of nutrients, it actually increases the excretion of many vitamins and minerals, most notably calcium. Alcoholism causes bone marrow toxicity and calcium loss that results in brittle bones and early osteoporosis, particularly in women. Alcohol-induced osteoporosis is a prime cause of broken bones in alcoholic patients.[5]

Simply put, just about everything the alcoholic does, nutritionally, is wrong. Calories are being ingested in the wrong form, nutrients are being malabsorbed and poorly utilized, and the foods that the alcoholic craves are precisely the ones that perpetuate the cycle of malnutrition.

Why can't the alcoholic simply change his or her eating patterns? If we told the alcoholic what he or she needed nutritionally couldn't the cycle be changed?

No.

The most important truth about alcoholism, the one fact that you must keep in the forefront of your mind at all times, is that the alcoholic is not capable of making rational choices. The malnutrition and toxicity of alcoholism are as damaging to normal brain function as a blow to the back of the head. The brain of the alcoholic is in no condition to process rational thought. In fact, it is barely capable of maintaining normal *physical* processes.

When I run across audiences who are skeptical of the relationship between alcohol's poisonous effects and the seemingly irrational, self-destructive behavior of so many alcoholics, I am reminded of the ill-fated Franklin expedition to the Canadian Arctic. This failed attempt to discover the fabled Northwest Passage proved, almost a century later, to be a classic example of the disastrous behavioral consequences of brain toxicity.

The expedition ships became marooned in the Arctic ice.

The crew members waited for spring and for the ice to melt. Spring arrived, but the ice remained.

When another year (and the deaths of Franklin and his top officers) had gone by, the remaining crew members abandoned the ships and set out across the ice for the open water a thousand miles south. They took with them the lifeboats, loaded with trinkets, writing desks, and other personal items with little survival value, as well as canned food. Not surprisingly, most of the crew died.

The expedition's inexplicable choice of provisions and their decision to set out for a destination a thousand miles away when a manned whaling station lay only 150 miles north have led many historians to conclude that the men were suffering from mass psychosis as a result of two years of icebound isolation.

Recently, a team of Canadian scientists journeyed to the site of the Franklin expedition. They exhumed the bodies of two of the crew members and performed extensive forensic tests on their tissues. Their findings? Bone samples from both corpses revealed astonishingly high levels of lead.

The Franklin expedition was one of the first to make use of large amounts of canned food. No one in the newly founded canning industry knew of lead's neurotoxicity or that lead cannot be excreted by the body once it is ingested. With each meal, the members of the Franklin expedition were taking in a hefty dose of one of the most potent of all poisons. By the end of two years, these men were deep in the throes of lead poisoning, complete with severe mental derangement. They were literally incapable of making rational choices.

The alcoholic is similarly incapacitated. While alcohol is not so severely neurotoxic as lead, its effects are so widespread and pernicious that nearly every system in the body is drastically affected.

NEUROENDOCRINE EFFECTS

The neurotransmitter deficits outlined in chapter 4, when coupled with wide variations in blood glucose levels, lead to a pattern of severe mood swings in many alcoholic patients. In hundreds of clinical tests over the past twenty years it has been found that between 60 and 90 percent of individuals with alcoholism are depressed, with symptom patterns that match those of depressed patients without alcoholism.[6] Unlike primary depressives, however, alcoholics tend to slip in and out of depression with startling rapidity. This cycling *or switching* of symptoms often results in their being mistakenly diagnosed as manic-depressives. In actual fact, these seemingly random swings between elation and despair are linked to drastic shifts in serum glucose levels which alternately flood and deprive the brain of needed fuel.

Disturbed glucose metabolism has also been linked to low levels of serotonin (a mood-regulating neurochemical) in alcoholic patients. Serotonin deficiency is known to be involved in depressive syndromes and may be one of the reasons for the high suicide rates—attempted and successful—among alcoholic patients. Several researchers have found a correlation between hypoglycemic responses to the glucose tolerance test; low serotonin levels; and the impulsive, violent behavior that is common in alcoholism.[7] These changes in glucose and serotonin levels may be a result of an alcohol-induced dysfunction of the suprachiasmatic nuclei, the tiny structures in the brain that are crucial to both supplying serotonin and regulating glucose metabolism.[8]

Alcohol is known to disrupt the normal processes of cell membranes—altering the normal flow of chemicals through cells[9]—and this disruption has serious consequences in many regions of the brain beyond the suprachiasmatic nuclei. In the cerebellum, for example, alcohol impairs the cells that normally control the integrated muscular functions needed for complex movement. The cerebellum coordinates muscle tone (including posture) and hand-eye movements. Disruption of the cerebellum is responsible for many of the more obvious physical signs of drunkenness, including the classic inability to walk a straight line. Cerebellar disruption is magnified by the toxic effects of vitamin B deficiency, a condition known as polyneuropathy. As the disease progresses, the brain of the alcoholic begins to atrophy, to shrink in size as the brain cells die from the combined effects of malnutrition and toxicity. These neurological catastrophes cause specific symptoms and behavior patterns that increase in severity over time, notably:

- burning and tingling in the legs and feet
- muscle weakness
- lack of coordination
- trauma from falls that often results in broken bones or further brain injury
- memory lapses
- confusion
- visual disturbances
- paranoia

- delusions
- palsied movements
- tremors
- psychosis
- seizures

The most severe manifestation of alcoholic brain damage, Wernicke-Korsakoff syndrome, is characterized by memory disturbances so severe that patients are completely incapable of learning and storing new information. These patients are unable to tell you where they live, who cares for them, or what they had for lunch. If introduced to a new person, they will forget that person's identity as soon as he or she leaves the room. The brain regions that process and store new information have been permanently impaired.

Alcoholism also impairs the regions of the brain that regulate sleep, so that alcoholic patients experience a "self-sustaining disregulation of sleep" that is characterized by decreased amounts of deep sleep and more frequent changes of sleep stages.[10] Simply put, the alcoholic sleeps less, and what little sleep he or she gets is not particularly refreshing.

While alcohol tends to remove sexual inhibitions in the individual who is not alcoholic, in the alcoholic it eventually causes a severe paradoxical reaction.[11] There is a significant decrease in the levels of luteinizing hormone, which stimulates the gonads. This decrease results in a wide range of sexual dysfunction in both men and women. Sexual response in all alcoholics is diminished. In males, firmness of erection decreases as blood alcohol level increases. In women, sexual arousal is dramatically impaired. Serum testosterone levels in male alcoholics are depressed, while endogenous estrogen levels increase—leading to possible testicular atrophy, impotence, and loss of sexual drive. In fact, alcoholism is the second leading cause of impotence in male patients, and a major cause of amenorrhea (loss of normal menstrual cycles) in females. In essence, alcoholism disrupts the balance of sexual hormones to such an extent that men become more feminine and women more masculine.

GASTROINTESTINAL EFFECTS

We have already discussed alcohol's damaging effects on the organs that digest, process, utilize, and store nutrients. These effects are accompanied by a wide range of symptoms[12] that are easily misdiagnosed or attributed to conditions other than alcoholism.

In the mouth, alcohol-induced vitamin B deficiencies cause the tongue to become atrophied and smooth, while calcium deficiency and the poor oral hygiene that is typical of alcoholics promotes cavities and gum disease.

In the esophagus, alcohol irritates tissues and damages the sphincter muscle between the esophagus and stomach. This leads to nausea, vomiting, and a backup of acidic stomach contents into the esophagus that causes chronic heartburn. Blood flow through the veins of the esophagus is often impeded, causing enlarged veins that are easily broken or ruptured (particularly during vomiting).

In the stomach, gastric irritation causes alcoholic gastritis— characterized by painful burning sensations, usually occurring early in the day. The lining of the stomach can become so badly damaged that peptic ulcers and severe internal bleeding develop.

In the intestinal tract, the combination of poor diet and alcohol-induced membrane damage can lead to chronic diarrhea that drastically alters the alcoholic's electrolyte balance, sometimes causing severe dehydration.

In the pancreas, alcohol's effect on protein synthesis results in a buildup of pancreatic enzymes that actually begin to digest the cells of the pancreas itself. This process, known as pancreatitis, results in severe pain in the upper abdomen, accompanied by vomiting, abdominal muscle spasms, and other symptoms. Pancreatitis is but one of the many life-threatening illnesses spawned by alcoholism.

In the liver, alcohol's effects are the most dramatic and deadly. The liver is the body's central processing plant. As such, it bears the brunt of alcohol's onslaught. Alcoholic liver disease is one of the major causes of death in this country for males between the ages of twenty-five and sixty. In the early stages of the disease (alcoholic fatty liver), fat, protein, and water accumulate within the liver cells, impairing normal liver function. As the disease progresses the liver cells become inflamed (alcoholic hepatitis), and finally begin to die off (alcoholic cirrhosis) so that blood is no longer able to flow through the diseased and dying cells.

CARDIOVASCULAR EFFECTS

Small doses of alcohol produce increases in heart rate, cardiac output, blood pressure, and vasoconstriction. Over time, these changes can lead to a variety of serious cardiovascular complications,[13] including:

- cardiomyopathy, in which alcohol causes cellular damage to the cardiac muscle, eventually leading to the development of congestive heart failure
- cardiac rhythm disturbances, including "holiday heart," in which the heart alternately races and skips beats
- hypertension
- coronary artery disease, in part caused by the disorders of lipid metabolism that promote high cholesterol levels and inefficient clearance of of lipids from the blood

IMMUNOLOGICAL EFFECTS

The human immune system is marvelously complex—not a single system, really, but a vast network of responses to the various organisms, bacteria, and traumas that regularly threaten the body. The immune system has extensive links to almost every organ, particularly those of the gastrointestinal tract and the neuroendocrine system. Any threat or perceived threat to the body—from an unrecognized food protein to a near-miss on the freeway—can bring about some sort of immune response.

This responsiveness is a double-edged sword, however, since some immune responses do more harm than good. Most of the symptoms we experience with a head cold, for example, are the result of the immune system trying to expel the offending virus. The phlegm, sneezing, and coughing are all the end products of the immune system's massive assault on the alien invader. In some patients, particularly the very old and the very young, the body's response to a flu virus can actually be fatal. The great flu pandemic of 1918-1919, for example, is estimated to have cost 15 million lives.

When you are vaccinated against the flu or any other disease, the vaccine is actually a lesser form of the disease virus. The purpose of the vaccination is to introduce your immune system to the virus and provoke a mild response. If you should later come in contact with the actual virus, the immune response will not be as violent and debilitating. Simply put, vaccinations teach the body to kill off the virus without also killing you.

For reasons that are still unclear, the immune system can also become activated against the cells of the body itself. In these autoimmune disorders the immune system reacts to benign cells of the body as if they were hostile invaders. In the disease systemic lupus erythematosus, for example, antibodies develop that attack the cells of the skin, joints, kidneys, nervous system, and other organs. The symptoms of the disease can be as mild as a red rash or as severe as debilitating arthritis or psychosis. The exact cause, or causes, of this disease are unknown.

The flip side to autoimmune disorders occurs when the immune system fails to recognize and attack truly invasive organisms or cells. Immunodeficiency can be inherited (as in the cases of bubble babies who must be kept in an entirely sterile environment) or they can develop as the result of a virus or long-term stress on the immune system. The most dramatic example of an acquired immunodeficiency is acquired immune deficiency syndrome—or AIDS. And most cancers can be attributed to the failure of the immune system to recognize and destroy cancerous cells.

Alcohol, because it affects every system in the body, is capable of interfering with every aspect of these immune responses.[14] Alcoholic malnutrition—particularly deficiencies in protein, pyridoxine, and zinc—is involved in a general depression of immune function. Alcohol-induced damage to bone marrow, which is involved in the production of immune cells, further impairs immunological response; alcoholic liver disease kills off the cells in the liver, which normally regulate immunoglobulins and guard against toxins and bacteria.

As a result of these immunological impairments, alcoholics are much more susceptible to illness—from a minor head cold to salmonella—and their bodies are less able to repair themselves when damaged. In addition, the immune system of the alcoholic is less able to recognize and destroy cancerous cells.[15] This decreased cancer-fighting ability is one of the great dangers of alcoholism, since so many alcoholics live a life-style that exposes them to potent carcinogens—from nicotine to chemical preservatives to alcohol itself. Cancer—of the liver, lungs, pancreas, breast, cervix, throat, and all the organs of the digestive tract—is one of the primary causes of death among alcoholics.

Alcoholism not only suppresses necessary immune responses, it provokes counterproductive ones. Alcohol-damaged intestinal walls allow incompletely digested food proteins to pass into the bloodstream. It is thought that the immune system responds to these proteins as if they were antigens (invaders)—provoking an allergic response.[16] When tested for food allergies, alcoholics have consistently been found to be much more reactive than nonalcoholic patients, particularly to the ingredients commonly found in alcoholic beverages—grains, malt, and yeast.[17]

From a clinical perspective, this means that the alcoholic is routinely ingesting the very substances which provoke a negative immunological response. These food sensitivities have wide-ranging effects, from intestinal damage to mood swings, and also place considerable strain on the immune system. Even after being abstinent, the antibodies remain in the alcoholic's system, and the foods and substances which provoke an allergic response need to be avoided. After years of treating more than seventeen thousand alcoholic patients, it is my firm belief that the importance of food sensitivities has been grossly underestimated in alcoholic patients and that immune testing and restoration are crucial to successful recovery.

Acetaldehyde—the by-product of alcohol that causes so many biological problems—is also involved in disrupting immune function.[18] When acetaldehyde stays in circulation it is known to form chemical links with a variety of proteins and molecules. These adducts provoke an immune response which aggravates and perpetuates damage to the cells of the liver, further impairing the liver's ability to eliminate poisons from the body.

As you can see, the disease of alcoholism involves much more than simply drinking too much. The combined effects of malnutrition and toxicity are physiologically devastating. The alcoholic has gone through the metabolic equivalent of a train wreck, no matter how sturdy he or she may seem.

Repairing this train wreck will take much more than simply removing alcohol from the body. It will take complete biological restoration, as well as education and behavioral training. As we shall see, the abrupt removal of alcohol *without* such precautions and care can be fatal.

7

WITHDRAWAL

By now it should be abundantly clear that the person with alcoholism is suffering from something far more severe than a drinking problem. The biochemistry of the alcoholic has become so twisted, so dependent on the presence of alcohol for normal functioning, that giving up alcohol is about as easy to do as giving up breathing.

Well-meaning friends and family of alcoholics who do not understand this basic fact sometimes make the deadly mistake of trying to cure the alcoholic at home—by helping the alcoholic stop drinking cold turkey. The results of these home cures can be disastrous.

Several years ago I treated a man who had gone through such a cure. He was a well-to-do, articulate, and well-educated businessman with a long history of alcohol abuse. His friends decided to help him kick the habit once and for all by taking him to his seaside home and watching over him to be sure he did not drink. Several days into this program the man went into seizures. His friends, justifiably frightened, rushed him to the nearest hospital, where emergency procedures failed to arrest the seizures. When the physicians were finally informed of the man's alcoholism they transferred him to our facility.

We succeeded in arresting the seizures and administered medication and vitamin supplementation to counteract the hyperactivity of the autonomic nervous system that is a primary cause of withdrawal tremors, seizures, and hallucinations. Once the crisis was past, however, it became clear that something was terribly wrong.

The man's memory had been badly damaged. When I came into the room and introduced myself he was charming and cooperative, although he did not remember much of what had happened to him during his home cure. When I returned later in the same day, however, it was clear that he did not recall having met me. Other members of the treatment team had also noted that this patient—who had once been a brilliant businessman, capable of remembering complex stock information with ease—had lost all short-term memory. New information and experiences flowed out of his mind like water, leaving no trace.

This condition, known as Korsakoff's syndrome, was the result of the brain damage caused by prolonged seizures, as well as by the accumulated damage of years of alcoholism. Although some of the man's memory abilities returned over time, much of the damage could have been avoided entirely if he had been detoxified from alcohol in a hospital with strict medical supervision.

This tragic case illustrates the very grave risks involved in alcohol withdrawal and the importance of medical care during the withdrawal process. Although the severity of withdrawal can vary greatly depending on how long the person has been alcoholic, how much he or she drinks, the extent of physical and metabolic damage, and the individual's biochemistry, there is no real way to predict its course.

If left untreated, alcohol withdrawal can progress through, or stop at, any of four stages.[1] There is still some question about what, exactly, causes these physiological symptoms. In general, the syndrome is thought to be a result of hyperactivity of the autonomic nervous system. This hyperactivity is a rebound reaction to alcohol's depressant effects and occurs only after alcohol has been cleared from the blood for several hours to several days.

Stage one of alcohol withdrawal can occur from six to twelve hours after the alcoholic's last drink. It is characterized by a pattern of relatively mild symptoms that can be easily misdiagnosed as "hospital jitters" (in hospitalized patients with undiagnosed alcoholism) or an acute anxiety or panic attack. The most common signs of stage one withdrawal are:

- mild agitation
- anxiety
- restlessness
- tremors
- loss of appetite
- insomnia
- racing heartbeat
- high blood pressure
- sweating

Stage two withdrawal symptoms will usually manifest themselves within twenty-four hours of the last drink. Stage one symptoms will be present, along with hallucinations. These hallucinations are nothing like the pink elephants and other benign apparitions that cartoonists and comedians have portrayed over the years. The hallucinations of alcohol withdrawal affect all the senses, so that the alcoholic not only sees, but smells, hears, and feels these apparitions. And more often than not they are truly horrifying creatures such as gigantic bugs or snakes. A common and vivid withdrawal hallucination is that hundreds of bugs are crawling over or inside the alcoholic's skin. In between hallucinations the alcoholic may be perfectly lucid and well oriented, and not be able to recall the hallucinatory episodes.

Stage three alcohol withdrawal is characterized by the symptoms of stages one and two, along with seizures. In 40 percent of cases the seizures are acute, single episodes.

In *stage four* withdrawal, however, seizures are far more serious. Delerium tremens (or D.T.'s) is the most serious form of alcohol withdrawal, and can occur two to three days after the last drink. If the alcoholic is cross addicted to other drugs, symptoms may be delayed for up to ten days. Delirium tremens is a medical emergency, with a mortality rate of up to 20 percent. In fact, alcohol withdrawal is one of the few forms of drug withdrawal that can—and does—kill if left untreated.

Delirium tremens is characterized by the hallucinations and anxiety symptoms of stages one and two, with much more frequent seizures (sometimes continuous, as we saw in the earlier example), as well as:

- profound confusion
- disorientation
- fever
- very elevated blood pressure
- rapid pulse
- severely elevated heart rate

Alcoholics in withdrawal also lose essential body fluids at a tremendous rate, which disrupts electrolyte balance throughout the body and contributes to brain damage. Because of this, it is essential to monitor fluid and electrolyte balance at all times. In recovery, alcoholics may have a high blood volume but be paradoxically deficient in important electrolytes such as magnesium, zinc, potassium, and phosphates. For this reason, their electrolyte balance should be monitored very carefully, and these substances should be replenished in a way that does not overload the body's total fluid content (which can cause potentially fatal complications such as congestive heart failure).

During delirium tremens the alcoholic is usually so ill and potentially physically violent due to hallucinations that he or she is unable to take fluids or food by mouth, and intravenous drips must be instituted.

Alcohol withdrawal, particularly if it reaches the stage of delirium tremens, increases the risk of several other deadly conditions, most notably:

- stroke—caused by dramatically increased blood pressure and heart rate, which puts increased stress on veins and arteries that may already be damaged from alcoholism

- heart attack—caused by increased heart rate, pulse, blood pressure, and temperature that all put tremendous strain on the alcoholic's heart muscle, which may already be damaged by prolonged alcohol consumption; withdrawal causes irregularities in heartbeat that can result in complete cardiac shutdown
- permanent brain damage—caused by the seizures, dehydration, and electrolyte imbalances of withdrawal, when coupled with the malnutrition and toxicity of alcohol over time, can result in extensive brain cell death and permanent mental and physical impairment, particularly of memory and physical coordination

The most important thing to remember about alcohol withdrawal is that there is no way to predict the severity of the symptoms. No one, physician or layman, can anticipate the course of withdrawal, particularly since it is difficult to really know the extent of an alcoholic's drinking. Unless you are with the alcoholic twenty-four hours a day, every day, you cannot be sure how much alcohol the alcoholic consumes. For this reason, you should *never* attempt to detoxify the alcoholic at home without medical supervision.

Some people will tell you that cold turkey withdrawal is good for the alcoholic, that it will toughen him or her up and show them how bad alcohol really is. This attitude is ignorant, sadistic, and dangerous. Avoid such individuals like the plague.

8

THE DILEMMA OF DIAGNOSIS—DOCTORS

Consider these two scenarios:

A fifty-three-year-old woman climbs a stool in her kitchen to get a utensil from a closet over the sink. She falls and fractures her left wrist and ankle. She is rushed to the hospital and treated. She remains in the hospital for a week, receiving the best of modern trauma care. She returns home to recuperate. Three months later she dies from a fall down her cellar steps.

A fifty-six-year-old architect suddenly and with no apparent cause slits his wrists in a suicide attempt. He survives, is placed in a psychiatric facility and treated for agitated depression with therapy and Valium. Upon release he is placed on Valium maintenance and continued psychotherapy. Six months later he again slits his wrists and dies.

In both cases, the treating physicians missed one crucial causal element. They perceived the most obvious symptoms—broken bones and depression—without discovering the underlying cause—alcoholism.

The accident-prone woman was actually exhibiting the classic loss of muscular coordination and balance caused by alcohol-induced damage to the cerebellum. Her bones broke so easily because of unusually advanced osteoporosis—the result of malnutrition and bone marrow damage secondary to alcoholism.

The depressed architect, on the other hand, was an adult child of an alcoholic with a long history of alcohol abuse and mood swings. The Valium, which initially helped relieve the mood swings, quickly created a cross addiction which proved deadly when mixed with alcohol's depressant effects.

In both these patients, the signs and symptoms of alcoholism were there to be seen, if only the physicians had looked. But like so many doctors today, these physicians missed the forest for the trees, treating the symptoms while missing the cause.

Every physician working in the field of alcoholism has hundreds of true and tragic stories like these. They are the norm, not the exception.

In medicine, there is always a time lag between the discovery of a treatment or medication and when doctors actually put it into practice. The world of the research laboratory is very different from the world of applied medicine. Research results must be replicated, and new medicines and procedures safety tested before they are applied to patients.

In the case of alcoholism, however, this time lag has lasted more than thirty years *despite the fact that the research base for the biological nature of alcoholism has been well documented, often replicated, and is growing all the time.* Putting this knowledge into practice does not require new medicines or new procedures. In fact, the diagnostic and treatment tools that could prevent and cure alcoholism are already available to any doctor who chooses to use them.

Why are so few doctors making these diagnoses?

There are many reasons, but the three most easily quantified factors are: lack of proper training, restrictive insurance policies, and personal fears and prejudice.[1]

LACK OF PROPER TRAINING

The problem starts in medical school, where budding physicians are taught that alcoholism is basically a psychological problem (if they are taught about alcoholism at all) and that alcoholics have a personality disorder that promotes uncontrolled and destructive drinking. Because of this, medical students are taught to treat the medical effects of drinking—liver disease, broken bones, ulcers, pancreatitis, etc.—as separate entities. Alcoholism as a single, unique disease is not recognized. Little or no attention is paid to the considerable research evidence that has established alcoholism as a *biological,* as well as behavioral, disease.

When faced with alcoholic patients, in all their biological complexity, these physicians are basically at a loss. Despite the fact that they are products of one of the best medical establishments in the world, they have no useful definitions or guidelines to go by, and end up treating alcoholism by default, haphazardly handling medical crises as they arise.

Some of the specific educational stumbling blocks which prevent doctors from identifying and treating alcoholism are the following:

The Lack of a Comprehensive Definition of the Disease.
There are specific definitions for most diseases and disorders; definitions which include symptoms, general course, and treatment strategies. The definitions of alcoholism are all psychobehavioral, however, and do not even begin to address the true complexity and severity of alcoholism.

Confusion Over How Alcoholism Relates to Other Diseases. Because alcoholism is a contributing factor in so many of the other chronic diseases, doctors may experience confusion over what to handle first. These are the cases when "treatment by default" is most likely to occur. The physician will naturally be inclined to handle the disorder which is most easily defined. When faced with a hypertensive patient who is probably alcoholic, for example, many physicians will treat only the hypertension. Hypertension is understandable; they have been trained to diagnose and treat it as a disease with specific drug therapies. Alcoholism, on the other hand, is a mass of contradictory information and instructions.

Uncertainty Over the Limits of "Heavy Drinking." Not every person who drinks every day is an alcoholic. On the other hand, there are plenty of alcoholics who only drink beer. Physicians, like the general public, are hampered by the lack of an easy definition of "normal" as opposed to abusive or alcoholic drinking.

Under the best of circumstances, physicians are given only minimal training in nutrition and pharmacology. Because of this, the most subtle nutritional and neurochemical effects of alcoholism are easily misunderstood and readily discounted. Alcoholism is a disease of such complexity that it dramatically points up many of the deficiencies in modern medical training.

Most doctors, to their credit, are aware of these deficiencies and express a desire to learn more about alcoholism even as they admit to feeling unqualified to diagnose or treat it. Unfortunately, most insurers do little to encourage physicians to diagnose and treat alcoholism more effectively.

RESTRICTIVE INSURANCE POLICIES

At the beginning of this book I detailed the toll—economic, sociological, and medical—that alcoholism takes in this country. I also presented some rather depressing statistics on the effectiveness of most alcoholism treatment.

The people who set insurance and research policies are equally aware of these statistics, and make their decisions accordingly. Believing that alcoholism is a behavioral problem and that alcoholism treatment does not work, they set strict limits on the length of time that a person can be treated for alcoholism and on the number of times an alcoholic can be treated in one lifetime. The unstated assumption is that if the treatment does not work the first time, any additional treatment is simply throwing good money after bad.

These restrictive policies have a very distinct effect on the treatment choices of practicing physicians. When dealing with third party payment plans, most physicians will naturally tend to list the diagnosis that will ensure payment and have the least limitations. Few physicians are eager to go head-to-head with an insurance company, particularly when such confrontations may lead to being "red flagged" and waiting extended periods of time before being paid.

As a result, the patient with a bleeding ulcer and hypertension secondary to alcoholism who has used his "once in a lifetime" insurance allotment may not be encouraged to go in for further alcoholism treatment. His hypertension and ulcer will be treated, certainly. The doctor may even suggest that he attend Alcoholics Anonymous meetings. But that will be the extent of the treatment for his alcoholism.

PERSONAL FEARS AND PREJUDICES

Doctors are human. This rather obvious fact is frequently forgotten by patient and physician alike. Patients with alcoholism often bring out the less than ideal aspects of a physician's humanity.

Professionally, the alcoholic patient serves as a sharp reminder of the limits of a physician's knowledge and abilities. The physician can respond to this reminder in a number of ways.

- *Blaming the victim* is a natural outgrowth of the psycho-moral view of alcoholism. The physician blames the patient for becoming alcoholic and willfully continuing to drink despite the physician's orders not to.
- *Fear and withdrawal* from the patient if the physician feels that the alcoholism is untreatable and the patient is doomed.

- *Overt hostility* toward the patient, in an unconscious attempt to drive him or her away and thereby escape the responsibility of caring for an uncooperative and difficult patient.

In addition, there are purely personal factors which can determine the physician's response to the alcoholic patient.[2] For example:

- *The presence of alcoholism in the physician's family.* Depending on the circumstances, the physician may slip into responses learned while growing up in an alcoholic home.
- *Previous traumatic experience with alcoholic patients* can color the physician's expectations and response. This is particularly true of doctors who interned or trained in urban settings where they had extensive contact with patients on the extreme end of the alcoholic spectrum—homeless and indigent alcoholics.
- *Personal problems with alcohol or drugs.* Drug abuse and alcoholism are not uncommon in doctors, and a physician who is in the throes of alcoholism and denial is in no condition to diagnose or treat others with the disease.
- *Frustration* with the patient's denial of alcoholism. Denial is a fairly common phenomenon in medicine, but it is particularly severe in alcoholism. The alcoholic patient will do everything he or she can to find other explanations for his or her problems. Continually refuting these denials and

justifications can be frustrating in the extreme, particularly for physicians who are used to unquestioning obedience from their patients.

These factors, when combined, result in a unique and unfortunate pattern of attitudes and responses to the alcoholic patient. When presented with an alcoholic patient with minor or minimal medical problems (such as gastritis), the physician is likely to view the alcoholism as a purely behavioral problem. The patient is not given the consideration normally accorded a sick person, since he or she is not physically sick. The gastritis is treated, and the patient sent on his or her way. The alcoholism is the patient's responsibility, not the doctor's.

When this same physician is faced with a patient with advanced alcoholic hepatitis or cirrhosis, the attitude changes remarkably. *Now* the patient has something recognizably medical. Now the requirements for being a "sick person" have been fulfilled. Now the physician is on familiar ground and can treat the patient with sympathy and consideration. Of course, now the patient may be so far gone that he or she has suffered permanent and irreparable damage. But at least insurance will cover it.

All of these pitfalls can, and will, be avoided as medical schools institute courses and programs on alcoholism and physicians and insurers learn more about the true nature of the disease. Several major medical schools and teaching hospitals, most notably Johns Hopkins, have already begun such programs.[3] But it will be years before these changes take permanent hold. What about you, now? How are you going to identify and help your alcoholic loved one, before it is too late?

CASE STUDY:
More Than Depression

Mrs. G. was a sixty-five-year-old woman who had been referred by her psychiatrist for admission to our psychiatric hospital. For the previous eighteen months she had been receiving outpatient treatment for depression and anxiety. She was being maintained on Mellaril (a powerful antidepressant medication) and 20 milligrams of Valium a day. Despite these measures, her condition had become markedly worse.

At the time of her admission, Mrs. G. had been diagnosed as suffering from a severe affective disorder and agitated depression. Her referring psychiatrist recommended that she be admitted for inpatient evaluation and possibly shock therapy to relieve her depression.

On the surface, Mrs. G. presented a fairly classic picture of reactive depression. Her husband had died approximately two years before, and over the past few months she had experienced a lack of interest in herself, her surroundings, her relatives, and life in general. She had essentially stopped cooking for herself and was relying on prepared and fast foods since the death of her husband. The marriage had been a long and happy one, and she was having considerable difficulty living without her spouse.

Physically, Mrs. G. complained of tremendous fatigue, accompanied by loss of appetite, sleeplessness, and an inability to concentrate. She stated that she was losing her hair, that her feet and legs were often numb and/or tingling, and that she was always tense and anxious. On the occasions when she had stopped taking Valium, these symptoms became worse.

When asked about her drinking history and whether she ever took more Valium than was prescribed, Mrs. G. firmly denied any extra Valium use and indicated that she was, at most, a light social drinker. Although she was feeling very depressed and hopeless, she denied having any thoughts of suicide.

At first glance, all of Mrs. G.'s symptoms were consistent with a diagnosis of depression. The physical exam revealed a woman who—despite a reportedly poor dietary intake—was twenty pounds overweight, with pallid, pasty skin and a sensory deficit in her legs and feet. Otherwise, her physical condition was not remarkable.

Laboratory tests, however, told a very different story. Mrs. G.'s blood tests revealed that her red blood cells were enlarged and misshapen, and that her liver enzymes were markedly elevated. Both these findings were compatible with alcoholic liver disease. Her total protein level was quite low, and vitamin and mineral assays revealed considerable nutritional deficits, particularly of thamine and the other B vitamins, vitamin A, magnesium, potassium, phosphate, calcium, and zinc.

Mrs. G. also reported frequent episodes of runny nose, as well as occasional hives and asthma attacks. An allergy screen revealed a general increase in immune reactivity, with particular sensitivity to house dust mites, molds, and grains (particularly wheat, yeast, corn, and oats).

A routine toxic metal screen revealed on alarming and baffling finding. Mrs. G. had a marked elevation in her lead level. We repeated this test several times, and performed additional studies which confirmed that not only was Mrs. G.'s lead level elevated, she was also suffering from early lead toxicity.

These findings shed new and contradictory light on Mrs. G.'s condition. Despite her claim of being only a social drinker, her lab results were those of a long-term heavy drinker with early liver disease and severe malnutrition. The neuropsychological effects of her alcoholism were being aggravated by her lead toxicity and were only masked and/or worsened by the other psychiatric drugs she had been receiving. While Mrs. G. may indeed have had some psychological problems, it was impossible to address them until she had been detoxified and physically rehabilitated.

I confronted Mrs. G. in as firm, gentle, and concerned manner as possible. I showed her the test results and explained what they meant, and again asked her about her drinking pattern. At first she denied it, became angry and tearful, and said she wanted to leave the hospital. I held fast, explaining to her that she might try to fool herself, her family, even me, but she could not fool her body. She was very ill and would only become more ill if she did not receive treatment.

Mrs. G. finally admitted that she had been drinking heavily for a long time, and that lately her drinking had increased. She stated that she was drinking well before her husband's death and that she had begun to feel depressed before he passed away. At this point her alcohol intake had reached the equivalent of a pint of ninety proof alcohol a day.

Her parents had been teetotalers, but further questioning revealed that their abstinence was a reaction to her paternal grandfather's florid and fatal alcoholism. She herself had begun drinking late in life, and had only become a heavy drinker in the last five or so years.

We had yet to explain Mrs. G.'s lead toxicity, however. Studies performed on her home revealed that lead was leaking into Mrs. G.'s drinking water (which came from a drilled well). The board of health confirmed this and began measures to decontaminate her water supply while she was receiving inpatient treatment.

Mrs. G. was admitted to our alcoholism treatment unit, not our psychiatric hospital, where she was detoxified from alcohol, Valium, and Mellaril. She was under medication for her alcohol withdrawal for the first three days, and maintained on medication to ease her Valium withdrawal for three weeks. (Valium takes considerably longer to clear from the body.)

During this period we administered nutrient supplementation both orally and intramuscularly for the first three days and proceeded to teach Mrs. G. how to maintain proper nutrition and avoid the foods to which she was allergic. More extensive testing was performed after she was stabilized, and immunotherapy was instituted.

After two weeks of inpatient treatment, Mrs. G.'s psychological and physical symptoms were much relieved, but it was clear that she had never fully worked through her grief over her husband's death. Additional psychological counseling was provided to help her resolve these issues and construct a plan for her new life.

After about a month of inpatient treatment, Mrs. G. left the hospital and returned to her now lead-free home. She became extremely active in her local AA group, and rediscovered her old joy of cooking, both for herself and her friends. She stayed involved with a grief therapy group, and continued in contact with my office for regular checkups and immunotherapy. For the first time since before her husband had died, she felt like a whole, functional person.

Imagine, if you will, what would have happened to this intelligent, vibrant woman if we had taken her psychiatric profile at face value and not further investigated her physical condition: hospitalization, increased levels of psychoactive medications, worsening malnutrition, perhaps deepening depression and electroshock treatments. But in the case of this "psychiatric patient" the problem was far more than depression.

9
IDENTIFYING THE ALCOHOLIC

If you are reading this book, you are probably concerned that someone you know and love may be an alcoholic. Perhaps the problem is so obvious and severe that you have absolutely no doubts about the condition. Or perhaps you only suspect alcoholism and need a way to be certain.

There are a lot of myths about what defines an alcoholic. An alcoholic is someone who drinks every day. An alcoholic is someone who gets drunk a lot. An alcoholic is someone who drinks lots of hard liquor.

In reality, none of these things are necessarily sure signs of alcoholism. Not all alcoholics drink every day, and not everyone who drinks every day is alcoholic. Alcoholics generally don't get falling down drunk until the late stages of the illness. And there are plenty of alcoholics in the world who drink only wine or beer.

On the other hand, it is possible to abuse alcohol without

being an alcoholic. Alcohol is a powerful drug, and it is possible to use it unwisely even if not addicted. The college student who gets "faced" on homecoming weekend and then goes joyriding is abusing alcohol. The businessman who comes home from work and drinks four martinis before dinner to avoid talking to his wife is abusing alcohol. But neither one is necessarily alcoholic. Anyone can occasionally be foolish or reckless in their use of alcohol and hurt themselves or others.

What sets the alcoholic apart from the rest of the drinking population are the biochemical changes that result from drinking and which make alcohol a biological imperative, not a social option, for these people.

Physicians can detect the physical and biochemical presence of alcoholism by performing sophisticated lab tests and analyses. Those of us without such equipment must rely on other clues and observe the entire pattern of behavior in the suspected alcoholic. Since we now know that alcoholism goes far beyond merely drinking too much, we must look for behaviors and habits that are associated with all the aspects of alcoholism—from nutritional to neurological. The following twelve questions cover most of the hallmarks of alcoholism.

1. *Has this person stopped eating regular meals?* Irregular eating patterns and skipped meals are the norm in alcoholic persons. Alcohol is the main source of energy and calories.
2. *Has this person been eating more sugar and sweets?* Alcoholics use sugar to counteract the drops in blood sugar that follow alcohol consumption.

3. *Has he or she inexplicably gained weight recently?* The empty calories of alcohol and other sugary foods frequently lead to overweight even as they cause malnutrition.

4. *Is he or she able to drink without seeming intoxicated?* The biochemical changes in the liver of the alcoholic, particularly the MEOS, make it possible for the alcoholic to drink a great deal without outward effect.

5. *Has he or she recently increased the amount he or she drinks?* Although it increases tolerance, the MEOS also requires progressively greater amounts of alcohol in order to function, and the alcoholic needs more and more alcohol in order to feel any effect.

6. *Does he or she drink every day, and is there a regular pattern to this drinking?* As the addiction progresses, the alcoholic needs to maintain a constant blood alcohol level in order to feel even vaguely normal or be able to function.

7. *Has he or she begun to exhibit mood swings?* The dramatic drops in blood glucose level and the disruption of normal brain chemical balance lead to dramatic emotional and psychological peaks and valleys for the alcoholic.

8. *Has he or she begun to react inappropriately to relatively common events*—in particular, with aggression? Alcohol-induced changes in neurochemistry result in a relaxation of impulse control and an increase in aggressive responses.

9. *Has he or she been depressed or mentioned suicide?* The hypoglycemic and neurochemical responses that cause mood swings and encourage aggression also cause acute and severe depressive episodes.

10. *Has he or she lost interest in sex?* Alcoholism drastically affects the hormones and brain regions that regulate sexual activity, causing impotence and loss of sexual drive.

11. *Has he or she been more clumsy of late,* falling or dropping things? Alcohol impairs the higher brain functions that coordinate complex movement and control balance and posture.

12. *Has he or she been experiencing sleep disturbances,* including restless sleep and insomnia? Alcohol disturbs the brain regions that regulate sleep, leading to a pattern of restless and limited sleep time.

If you were able to answer yes to seven or more of these questions, you are probably dealing with an alcoholic. If you are still unsure, try answering the following twenty-three questions. These questions—pulled from the Michigan Alcoholism Screening Test (MAST)[1]—deal more directly with drinking behaviors and have been found to be highly accurate in identifying alcoholics in hospital situations. The number of points to be scored for each *yes* answer is in parentheses at the end of each question.

1. Does he or she feel he is a normal drinker? (2)
2. Has he or she ever forgotten events that occurred when he or she was drinking? (2)
3. Have his or her spouse or parents complained about his or her drinking? (1)
4. Can he or she easily stop drinking without a struggle after two drinks? (2)

5. Does he or she ever apologize or feel bad about his or her drinking? (1)
6. Do his or her friends and relatives consider him or her a normal drinker? (2)
7. Does he or she ever try to limit his or her drinking to certain times of day or certain places? (0)
8. Can he or she stop drinking at will? (2)
9. Has he or she ever attended an AA meeting? (5)
10. Has he or she gotten into fights when drinking? (1)
11. Has his or her drinking created marital problems? (2)
12. Have any of his or her family members gone to Al-Anon or similar groups? (2)
13. Has his or her drinking caused problems at work? (2)
14. Has he or she lost a lover because of his or her drinking? (2)
15. Has he or she lost a job because of his or her drinking? (2)
16. Has he or she been absent from work or school for more than two days in a row because of drinking? (2)
17. Does he or she drink before noon? (1)
18. Has he or she ever had liver trouble? (2)
19. Has he or she ever had tremors, hallucinations, or D.T.'s after heavy drinking? (2)
20. Has he or she ever gone for counseling over his or her drinking? (5)
21. Has he or she ever been hospitalized for alcoholism? (5)
22. Has he or she ever been hospitalized in a psychiatric facility when drinking was the cause? (2)
23. Has he or she ever been arrested for drinking-related behavior, including drunk driving? (2)

A score of five points or more indicates that the person is indeed alcoholic and needs treatment as soon as possible for the disease.

In theory, I should end this book right here. Armed with the results of these quick quizzes, you should be able to go tell the alcoholic that he or she is sick and drive him or her to the nearest hospital.

Unfortunately, alcoholism does not work that way. Even if you can find a good treatment program that is able to immediately admit the alcoholic, you will undoubtedly have a hard time convincing the alcoholic to go.

No one wants to admit their mortality. In almost every disease, the patient goes through a period of feeling that "it can't happen to me." In alcoholism this phenomenon—called *denial*—reaches new extremes and often infects the family and friends of the alcoholic as well. If you really wish to help the alcoholic, you must get to know the dynamics of denial in all its forms.

10

THE DILEMMA OF DIAGNOSIS—PATIENTS AND FAMILIES

I first saw Tony Simmons when he was thirty years old. He was the child of a family of lawyers and judges on Long Island. He himself had a degree in criminology from a prominent university and had risen quickly through the ranks of the police department to the rank of lieutenant in the detectives' division. Careers in law and law enforcement seemed to run in his family. So did alcoholism.

At the time we met, Tony was severely jaundiced with severe alcoholic hepatitis. He had been hospitalized for over a month and almost died on several occasions. Tony's liver was so severely damaged that it was impairing his blood's ability to clot properly, and he had frequent episodes of severe internal bleeding.

Despite the fact that Tony's liver was all but destroyed from alcoholism, Tony steadfastly denied having any problem with alcohol. He insisted that his liver problems were an inherited "weakness"—since both his father and grandfather had died of liver disease—and had nothing to do with his drinking habits. He felt that since he had a good head for liquor and was rarely drunk he could not possibly be an alcoholic. He held to this conviction even when reminded that he had been drinking up to a fifth of ninety proof alcohol a day for over two years. It was only intense pressure from his wife and family that persuaded Tony to remain in treatment after the initial crisis of his hepatitis was past.

Tony remained sober for four months after release from our rehabilitation program. He than began drinking just as heavily as before (because he could "take it"), and eventually landed in intensive care once again. Another stint of inpatient rehabilitation did nothing to reduce his denial, and over the course of the next five years he continued to drink. During this time his wife divorced him, winning custody of the children, the police department put him on permanent disability because of his liver disease, and his health continued to deteriorate.

At age thirty-five, Tony Simmons was admitted to our intensive care unit once again. His liver was practically nonfunctional. The buildup of toxins in his system had disordered his brain function, so that he was barely lucid at the time of admission. He was jaundiced. His legs and arms had shriveled into pipe stems. His abdomen was grossly distended from the buildup of fluids which his liver could no longer process. He was constantly nauseated, vomited often, and was suffering from internal bleeding that required several blood transfusions. And he still insisted that he was not alcoholic.

After a week of intensive care, during which he almost died on several occasions, Tony was stable enough to be transferred to a general ward before once again being admitted for long-term rehabilitation.

Although Tony was under nursing supervision while on the ward, he did have access to a phone. A few days into his stay on the ward he apparently persuaded a friend to bring him a bottle of vodka. He was found unconscious with the empty bottle in his bed.

Tony went into total liver failure with massive internal bleeding. Despite all our efforts, he died within a day—a thirty-five-year-old casualty of alcoholism who never once admitted having the disease.

At one point during his treatment, Tony gave me a beautiful miniature rocking chair which he had made while in the hospital. I keep that chair in my office as a constant reminder of how much we have yet to learn about the disease of alcoholism. In the five years I knew and treated Tony Simmons, I was never able to unravel the denial that locked his mind or to figure out the process that led him to literally drink himself to death.

Of the many cases of alcoholic denial that I have encountered, this was certainly one of the most severe. But after years of treating patients with alcoholism I am still amazed at how firm and entrenched denial can be. Alcoholism may well be the only disease that tells its victims they don't have it, right up to the moment it kills them.

Alcohol addiction strives to maintain itself. The body literally needs alcohol, and the consequences of losing it are painful and terrifying. Once alcoholism is established, alcohol is not a source of pleasure, it is a biological necessity, a medicine that fends off horrible physical and mental symptoms. While alcoholics may not consciously realize this, they do "know it in their bones"—or, to be more exact, in their cells, particularly those of the brain.

Like the members of the Franklin expedition, alcoholics are no longer capable of rational survival choices. Just as the members of the Franklin expedition saw nothing odd in trying to cross a thousand miles of ice to open water, though a manned outpost was only 150 miles away, alcoholics see nothing abnormal in their drinking patterns. When their spouses, friends, or employers make comments or become angry about their drinking, alcoholics feel that they are being persecuted. They always have an explanation for their drinking behavior, a reason why they don't need to stop.

Most alcoholics, like most of society, do not believe that alcoholism is a disease. This delusion contributes to denial, since it encourages the alcoholic to view any criticism of his or her drinking as an insult, an implication that he or she is weak or out of control. Their knee-jerk reaction to this insult (reinforced by the biological need to keep the alcohol supply coming) is to insist that they can stop whenever they want—they just don't want to now.

Ironically and tragically, these justifications can be very convincing. So convincing, in fact, that the alcoholic's family and friends may believe them as well. It is this ripple effect of denial that feeds the unique dynamics of the alcoholic family.

Alcoholism is a family disease in more than a genetic sense. Just as the strain of maintaining an alcohol addiction takes an enormous biological toll on the body, the strain of living and interacting with an alcoholic takes an enormous emotional and psychological toll on the family.

It is in the nature of the family unit to try to maintain a balance, a homeostasis within which the members can live and interact. When one member of the family becomes impaired or dysfunctional, it is natural for the balance to shift. Duties are redistributed, responsibilities changed, emotional ties loosened.[1]

When a member of the family is alcoholic, other family members can respond by taking on one or many of the following roles:

- *the enabler*, who makes excuses to family, friends, relatives, and employers to help the alcoholic conceal his or her drinking and rescue him or her from the consequences of his/her behavior
- *the scapegoat*, who accepts the blame from the alcoholic for his or her drinking. The scapegoat is the target of the alcoholic's projections and usually bears the brunt of the alcoholic's abuse, but still continually tries to please the alcoholic
- *the compensator*, who tries to make up for the alcoholic's behavior through exceptional achievements and perfection, and strives to be as independent as possible
- *the opportunist*, who uses the alcoholic's behavior as an excuse for his or her own actions, and unconsciously does not want the alcoholic to recover

Once the roles have been cast, the plot of the tragedy of the alcoholic family is remarkably consistent. The "play" can be divided into seven basic scenes:

1. *denial*—in which the family refuses to acknowledge the existence or severity of the alcoholism

2. *isolation*—in which the family withdraws from normal social interactions in an attempt to hide the increasingly odd, frightening, or embarrassing behavior of the alcoholic member

3. *disorganization*—in which the alcoholic family member fails to fulfill his or her responsibilities within the family group

4. *resentment/anger/hostility*—in which the rest of the family begin to take up the slack for the alcoholic and become increasingly resentful of the alcoholic's inability to function; arguments, sometimes violent, are common

5. *reorganization*—in which a crisis (loss of job, arrest, etc.) causes the family to band together to "cope with the problem"—usually by rigidly concealing the alcoholic's behavior and becoming even more isolated; the alcoholism becomes a given that the family members tacitly assume will always be with them

6. *isolation (part II)*—in which the family members draw further and further apart from one another, and push the alcoholic more to the periphery of family relationships; sexual relationships, conversations, and shared responsibilities cease to exist and the family structure degenerates into one of "every man for himself"

7. *physical separation*—in which the alcoholic physically leaves the home; this separation can be the result of divorce, forced eviction, or death

Although life in the dysfunctional alcoholic family can be horribly painful and leave deep emotional scars, the patterns of a dysfunctional family are very hard to break.[2] If there is a long history of alcoholism on both sides of the family, family members will undoubtedly see nothing particularly wrong with the way they relate to the alcoholic. The dysfunctional family setup is the only one they have ever known.

The family of the alcoholic, like the alcoholic himself, may have a tremendous fear of tampering with the family structure. The homeostasis of the alcoholic family may be radically askew, but at least it is familiar. The roles have been cast, the script written, the direction taken. Any changes, such as the admission that something is amiss or even the recovery of the alcoholic, will mean that everyone has to learn a new part. This fear can be enormously strong and can blind the family of the alcoholic just as effectively as the disease blinds the alcoholic.[3] I have met hundreds of mothers, wives, sons, daughters, fathers, and husbands of alcoholics who insisted that their loved ones weren't *really* alcoholic, the problem was just temporary, that they had never seen them drunk, etc., etc.

Part of this phenomenon can be attributed to the fact that the family, like the alcoholic, like insurance companies, like many doctors, clergymen, and politicians, believes that alcoholism is a sort of moral degeneracy. They may wonder what they did to cause their loved one's alcoholism—an idea that is encouraged by the alcoholic's tendency to look for outside reasons for his or her drinking—and feel that the admission of the existence of alcoholism is equal to an admission of their own guilt.

These same individuals would not dream of blaming themselves for their loved one's diabetes or hypertension or cancer. They would do everything they could to get the person into treatment. That is why it is essential that you make it clear to both the alcoholic and his or her family that alcoholism is *not* a mental illness, not a moral failure, not a symptom of some underlying problem. It is a complex metabolic disorder that has very serious physical and behavioral consequences. And if left untreated it can cripple the family even as it can kill the alcoholic.

If you are, yourself, a member of an alcoholic's family, it is time for you to look fearlessly at your own place in the syndrome of alcoholism, to determine the role that you have taken on and the preconceptions you need to abandon. For while you may not be drinking, you are just as much a victim of this disease as the alcoholic. Fortunately, you are in a much better position, both physically and mentally, to help yourself.

But first you must convince the alcoholic to get the treatment he or she so desperately needs.

CASE STUDY:
"Just One Won't Hurt . . ."

George was a forty-four-year-old, highly successful investment banker. His career had treated him well, and at forty-four he was already a multimillionaire with a large home on several acres of prime Long Island real estate. He, his wife, and three children were all members of several prestigious clubs, and traveled frequently. In general, he was the embodiment of the American dream.

At the time George came to my office he had been suffering from increasing bouts of nervousness, agitation, and headaches. He said he was having difficulty concentrating, frequently lost his temper, and was losing his coordination. He was having trouble sleeping at night, and had noticed a marked decrease in his sexual drive. These symptoms had worsened over the last six months, and he was particularly concerned over the episodes of panic, anxiety, and despair he was experiencing.

George was terrified that all that he had accomplished was going to be lost to him. His chronic fatigue had become so severe that he could no longer run or play tennis, and the only thing that made it possible for him to get through each day was the Valium his family physician prescribed to relieve his stress. The Valium was originally prescribed for only occasional use in acute anxiety attacks, but as the anxiety became more frequent, so did the Valium. On a more mundane level, George had also noticed that he now had chronic postnasal drip.

George reported that his brother had a history of asthmatic bronchitis, and that two of his children had rather severe allergies. He himself did not have asthma but was suffering from chronic gastrointestinal upsets and "did not know what to eat anymore."

Physical exam showed slightly elevated blood pressure. George's nose was swollen and "boggy," and his gums were receding and tended to bleed when he brushed his teeth. Otherwise his physical condition was within normal limits.

His laboratory tests revealed that his red blood cells were enlarged and somewhat distorted, although his other tests, including liver function, were essentially normal. George's cholesterol level was elevated, however, and allergy testing revealed that he was sensitive to many foods—particularly grains, sugar, and coffee. His nutritional profile revealed many deficiencies—particularly of zinc, thiamine, calcium, potassium, and folic acid.

When George and I first met, he had reported a very light drinking pattern that did not quite match the evidence provided by his symptoms and his lab results. A more detailed diagnostic interview, using many of the questions outlined in chapter 8, revealed that he drank a great deal, often, and that this drinking was interfering with all levels of his life, particularly with his family.

George agreed to be admitted for detoxification from alcohol and Valium, and responded well, never showing anything more severe than stage 1 symptoms. He refused to go into the rehabilitation program, so he was released after detox and followed on an outpatient basis with weekly visits during the first month, then visits every two weeks for three months, and finally monthly visits for another year.

We developed a rotational diet for George, to avoid the foods which caused an allergic response and taught him the basics of proper nutrition and good eating habits. He was placed on an allergy-free vitamin supplement and encouraged to slowly return to tennis and jogging.

Within one month of his release from the hospital, George was symptom free and able to take up some of his old sports again. Within three months his tennis game was almost back to normal, and he was once again actively enjoying his life, his career, and his family.

Unfortunately, George's wife was not able to accept that George was alcoholic, and consistently refused to become involved in his treatment. I had a conference with her, explained the nature of alcoholism, and noted that since both George's uncle and grandfather had died of alcoholism, George was in a high-risk group from birth. I gave her a book I had written *(Wrong Diagnosis, Wrong Treatment)* and tried to impress upon her the importance of alcoholism as the real cause of George's physical and psychological problems. I told her that although George was in a relatively early stage of the disease, it would progress very rapidly and become even more life threatening if its course was not arrested. Unfortunately, she did not believe any of this.

As George's recovery progressed, his wife's skepticism became an increasing problem. At social functions she would complain aloud that it was "awfully odd" that he couldn't have "just one drink." George resisted her pressure to drink in social situations, but it became increasingly difficult. It was not made easier by his own refusal to participate in AA, which cut him off from an important source of support and encouragement.

At George's six-month checkup, he informed me that he was starting to drink an ounce and a half of alcohol a week, and that if he could not handle that, he would quit. Although he was entirely asymptomatic, I strongly advised him against drinking at all. He insisted he wanted to try, and we let the matter rest.

This man's decision weighed on me for two weeks, at which point I sent him a personal and confidential letter urging him to give up his plan of attempting controlled drinking. I enumerated the study results that showed controlled drinking was not possible for alcoholics, and once more explained the concept of progression. I have yet to get a reply from him.

George's case clearly illustrates the importance of involving the family in alcoholism treatment. If his wife (and children) had truly understood the disease of alcoholism, they could have provided George with much needed support and encouragement. Instead, his wife viewed George's sobriety as a sort of social stigma that he had to "get over" if they were to socialize normally. I can only hope that this tragic and false reasoning will not lead to further alcoholic degeneration for George, and the unhappiness of an alcoholic marriage for his wife and children.

11

GETTING INTO TREATMENT

Now that you know what alcoholism is and that your loved one is indeed suffering from this disease, you are faced with the formidable task of convincing the alcoholic to get treatment.[1]

There are people who will tell you that it is impossible to help alcoholics unless they are willing to help themselves, that alcoholics have to "hit bottom" before they can give up their addiction.

Don't believe it.

As we have seen, it is impossible for alcoholics to think clearly about their condition. If you wait too long to intervene, the alcoholic may hit bottom so hard that there can be no coming back up—he or she may be permanently disabled by alcoholic brain, liver, or other organ damage. Early recognition is not only possible in alcoholism, it is *essential*.

If you still doubt this, remember that you would never wait for a diabetic person to hit bottom, withholding treatment until after he or she has developed so many circulatory problems that a leg has to be amputated. Nor would you let a relative with pneumonia stay at home until his or her lungs gave out. Many sufferers from other illnesses want to deny the existence or severity of their diseases, but relatives, friends, and physicians are quick to convince them of the importance of prompt treatment.

Only in alcoholism do we find this dangerous belief that the sick person can only recover if he or she *wants* to get well. Only in alcoholism do we hold the victims personally responsible for the illness that ravages their bodies.

It is true that the treatment of any disease is more likely to succeed if the patient is a willing and active participant and that in alcoholism the patient has to actively learn a new way of life. But that learning can only happen after the patient has been physically rehabilitated.

The man or woman you are concerned about is acutely ill, unable to think rationally, and severely deluded about his or her condition. You will have to take very sharp measures if you want to cut through the fog of alcoholism and get this person into treatment.

For the sake of argument, let us say that you are the wife of an alcoholic. Your husband has become less and less supportive, is no longer able to perform sexually, and is moody and sometimes hostile. He has been having trouble at work and rarely comes home before midnight. When he is home, he drinks lots of beer, smokes cigarettes, and watches TV while eating doughnuts and potato chips. Conversations usually degenerate into arguments over his drinking and irresponsibility. Your children stay away from home and no longer bring friends to visit. You feel as if you are living in a private hell that has been designed around his drinking and that there is no way out. You sometimes wish he would just disappear or die, and then you feel guilty about the wish. Despite all this, you still call his office and report that he is ill on the mornings he is hung over, and feel it is your duty to clean up after him when he is sick, make apologies for him when he has been rude or unpleasant to your friends, and take over the household finances he has let slide.

It is important that you realize that although you are in no way responsible for your husband's alcoholism, you are supporting (or enabling) it every time you call his office, pay his bills, or clean up his mess. Each of these actions is like trying to put a Band-Aid on a severed artery. You are dealing with the symptoms and not facing the disease. Alcoholism is not broken promises, missed appointments, or failed lovemaking. It is the vast network of disorders that *cause* these symptoms.

Your husband is equally confused about this and will probably respond to your complaints with promises to be on time, pay the bills, mow the lawn, etc. Do not be sucked into a pointless debate about these issues. All too often, attempts at intervention turn into an endless spiral of accusations and justifications. Your anchor in all of this must be the knowledge that alcoholism is a physical disease and that your husband will certainly die before his time if he does not receive medical care quickly. No matter what he says, no matter how hard he tries to sidetrack you, never let go of this central reality.

Even if your husband is willing to admit that he may have a drinking problem, he may well proceed to give you various reasons why he cannot do anything about it at the moment. Some of the reasons may even seem logical: I can't afford to leave my job. Our insurance won't cover it. The kids need braces. Who will take care of the backyard? My boss won't understand, and I'll be fired.

If you find yourself being swayed by these arguments, think of what you would do if you found out he had leukemia or some other illness. Would you allow him to put off going into the hospital until it was more convenient? Would you wait a couple of months to see if the disease went away by itself? Would you let him stay home and take care of it himself because chemotherapy was too expensive?

As a matter of fact, lack of money is the alcoholic's prime argument against getting treatment, so be prepared. Your husband will probably respond to the suggestion that he go into the hospital with as much horror as if you suggested he shave his head and give all his money to the Ayatollah Khomeini. Hospitalization is too expensive; he can't take the time; what do you think, that he's made of money? This will be particularly true if he is still functioning fairly well at work, since he will see no reason for taking a leave from his source of income.

On the surface, his objections may seem valid. What *will* you do if he loses his job? How *will* you cope with the hospital bills if his insurance doesn't cover the full cost of treatment? You should consider these questions and do your homework before confronting your husband. Find out the extent of his insurance coverage. Investigate the billing policies of local treatment facilities. Assess your own financial resources and options. Don't let him blindside you with a barrage of financial objections. Be armed with facts and figures and be ready to counterattack.

Remember, the cost of alcoholism treatment is certainly

going to be less than the cost of a long, slow death from liver disease. Or the cost of a funeral.

Ultimately, the thing most likely to propel your husband into treatment is being faced with a firm ultimatum. Because he is literally incapable of dealing with shades of gray, the choice must be between black and white, life and death, alcohol and you.

It's a little like the classic choice between the lady and the tiger. You need to present your husband with two doors: one leading to treatment and a healthy, sober life (the lady), and the other leading to complete separation from you and the others he loves and continued alcoholic degeneration (the tiger). There are no alternative ways out.

The frightening and difficult part of this for you is the fact that you must be willing to follow through on your ultimatum. If he refuses to get help, you must be ready, willing, and able to act on your promises. If you say you will divorce him, you should be prepared to do so. If you say you will leave the house, be packed and ready to go. If you say you will never again call his office for him or help him up when he falls, you must be prepared to stay away from the phone and to leave him lying in the street.

If you have been enabling him, it is likely he will not believe that your ultimatum is real until he actually sees you leave or is left lying in his own vomit. It is possible that he will delay making his choice between the lady and the tiger until after he has felt the first nips of the tiger's teeth. You must be willing to let him get a taste of the consequences of a life with alcohol as his only friend.

Obviously it would be better not to take such drastic measures—to present your case to your husband and then drive him to the treatment facility of your choice. While it is doubtful that it will ever be that easy, there are certain steps you can take to increase your chances of success.

Do Your Homework. First, contact your local Al-Anon chapter and get support for yourself. Attend meetings, learn all that you can about your own feelings and needs, and get advice and support on how to confront your husband. Then check out all the logistics of getting your husband admitted. Investigate treatment facilities, find out about insurance and payment plans, make certain that beds are actually available. When you've found one or more facilities that seem appropriate, pay them a visit before hand if possible. Know what you will be getting your husband into so that you can be an active part of his recovery process.

Enlist the Help of Others. There is power in numbers. If your husband is confronted with several people he knows, loves, and respects, all of whom feel that he is in deep physical and psychic trouble, he will have a much more difficult time denying his problem. Be certain that everyone involved understands the true nature of the disease of alcoholism and the risks involved. Make sure that every member of your intervention team is willing to act on their part of the ultimatum and play their part in closing all doors except the one that leads to treatment. Most important, make it very clear that this is not the Spanish Inquisition. You are not gathering together a jury to rebuke your husband for his failings or list the horrible things he has done while under the influence of alcohol. You are bringing together a group of people who love him and want to convince him of how desperately ill he really is.

Be Ready to Take Whatever Action Is Necessary. If you are successful in convincing your husband that he is alcoholic, you should be prepared to have him admitted for treatment that same day. Don't put admission off and give him time to once again build up his fortress of denial. Once the walls are down you must be ready to move in and occupy the territory before alcohol can try to take over again. On the other hand, if he still refuses to acknowledge his disease, you and the other members of the team should immediately follow through on your ultimatum, making it clear that you are willing to come back and support him completely *if he goes for treatment* but not before.

I cannot stress enough the importance of this "tough love" aspect of intervention. It can be astonishingly difficult, and you may feel that you are being heartless, cruel, or unfeeling in carrying through your ultimatum, but it is the only way to make the alcoholic face the reality of his disease. Do not lose sight of the fact that you are not responsible for this man's disease, and that many of the things you did to help him were actually hindrances.

As an example of such tough love—and its consequences—I would like to present you with the story of one of my patients, an aerospace engineer whom I shall call Jonathan.

Jonathan was forty-two, a truly brilliant engineer, and the son of an alcoholic. He and his wife, Carole, met in college when they were both working on their bachelor's degree. Carole now worked as an art director for a major magazine.

They had two children, both girls, Tara, aged nine, and Christine, aged twelve.

Jonathan had always been a hard drinker. In fact he had always prided himself on his ability to hold his liquor better than his peers, and enjoyed being able to have three martinis at lunch and still put in a good afternoon's work.

Over a period of about two years, however, Carole had become nervous about the frequency of these three martini lunches. They had been at several parties where Jonathan actually became drunk and abusive to some of his co-workers. Carole noticed that he no longer stopped at two predinner drinks, and his after-dinner drink had gone from a snifter of brandy to several shots of bourbon. On the few occasions that Carole jokingly asked Jonathan about his new drinking habits he became surly and curt, telling her to mind her own business. If he couldn't relax in his own home where could he relax?

Jonathan began to have trouble sleeping and would pace around the living room for hours on end, finally falling asleep only a few hours before he had to leave for work. He began to be late, and would come home complaining of headaches and stomach pain, which he blamed on the combined effects of the stress of his job and Carole's cooking.

One Saturday Carole overheard their younger daughter telling a friend that she couldn't stay for dinner because "my mommy doesn't like company." When Carole asked the child why she had said such a thing, Tara looked embarrassed and scared, and finally said that she didn't want her friends to meet her father because "he's gotten so mean."

The next day, Carole told Jonathan about the incident, hoping that it would make him feel guilty about his behavior and change. It didn't.

Instead, Jonathan (who had already had several scotches) became enraged at their ingratitude toward him, who worked so hard to keep food on the table and a roof over their heads. He furiously announced that if that was how they felt he would just eat elsewhere and save them all the trouble.

Carole, pushed to the breaking point, responded just as angrily, berating him for his lack of responsibility, his failure as a lover and husband, his inability to even be a proper father.

The fight escalated to the point that Jonathan put his fist through the hollow-core door of the kitchen and Carole ordered him out of the house. Jonathan went, breaking a glass pane on the front door as he slammed it shut.

After Jonathan had gone and Carole had calmed the two girls (who had been watching the entire incident from the stairs, in complete terror), she went to the phone book and called the number listed for Al-Anon. Shaking and tearful, she found out where the nearest meeting was that night.

Carole cleaned up the broken glass, fed the children, and prepared to go to the meeting, listening nervously for Jonathan's return. After dropping Tara and Christine at a friend's home, Carole went to her first Al-Anon meeting. It was an awakening. For the first time, Carole admitted to herself and others that her husband was an alcoholic and that she did not know how to handle it. She tearfully recounted the day's events, her fears for herself and her children, and her complete uncertainty of what to do. The other members of the group were supportive and informative, and gave her the names and addresses of several nearby treatment programs. Most important, they began to teach her what she would need to do to get Jonathan into treatment.

Carole left the meeting with a renewed sense of purpose and hope. Though she was still fearful, she now had the numbers of several people who were willing to be called at any time. She picked up the girls and returned home to wait for her next confrontation with Jonathan.

Jonathan did not come home that night. Terrified, Carole called around to many of their friends and relatives, and in the process told them of how serious Jonathan's alcoholism had become and how worried she was about him. Jonathan's mother and brothers were equally concerned. His older brother, Tom, himself a recovering alcoholic who remembered all too vividly their father's death from alcoholism, told Carole that they would need to perform an intervention if they were to get Jonathan into treatment.

Jonathan spent the night making the rounds of several area bars, and finally fell asleep near a small pond in a park near his home. He awoke stiff, sore, and dirty and arrived at work an hour and a half late for his mid-year review. His supervisor had been particularly concerned about Jonathan of late, and had tried to impress upon him how important this review was. After waiting forty-five minutes, the supervisor canceled the review and left a message with Jonathan's secretary that Jonathan should see him as soon as he got in.

Jonathan halfheartedly tried to clean himself up and went into the supervisor's office. The supervisor took one look at Jonathan's disheveled state and gave up any thoughts of giving him yet another chance to redeem himself. He informed Jonathan that his services would no longer be needed.

Shortly after Jonathan left the office for the final time—heading for his favorite bar because he "needed a drink"—Carole called. His secretary, embarrassed but truthful, told Carole what had happened.

Carole was stunned by this blow, and promptly called Jonathan's eldest brother. She was distraught, blaming herself for Jonathan's being fired, sure that if she had not "picked a fight" with him he would still have a job.

Tom, with a wisdom born of both his father's lost battle with alcoholism and his own recovery, quickly brought Carole off the track of guilt and self-blame. He reminded her that Jonathan's job performance had been sliding for some time, and that he would have been fired eventually. Most important, he told her that she could only be responsible for her own actions, not Jonathan's, and that her primary responsibility was to herself and the children, if Jonathan would not go for help. Then he gave her my number.

Carole called my office and I talked to her at some length about Jonathan's condition and our program. It was obvious that she was herself in great distress and that the situation was at a crisis point. Left unchecked, Jonathan could easily become a statistic.

I told Carole that we could admit Jonathan immediately, if she could get him to come in. My office manager contacted the admissions office to arrange the necessary paperwork, and got Carole and Jonathan's insurance information over the phone. There were several limitations in Jonathan's coverage, but our billing office indicated that a time payment schedule could be arranged. The crucial thing was to get Jonathan into the hospital as fast as possible.

By the time Jonathan arrived home that night, Carole was ready for him. Rather than subject the children to any further scenes, she had sent them to a friend's for the night.

Carole kept admirably calm throughout her confrontation with Jonathan, despite her horror at his dilapidated appearance. She told him very simply that she now realized that he was an alcoholic and that he needed treatment. She apologized for some of the vicious things she had said earlier, since she now realized that he really wasn't in control of his own mind or body any longer. And she told him, quite firmly, that if he would not go into the hospital to get treatment for his disease he would have to leave the house and stay away from her and their daughters. She loved him, but she could not live with his disease any longer.

Jonathan hotly denied being an alcoholic and told her it was all in her head, that he was just having a rough time at work. Carole countered with the fact that she had spoken to his mother and brothers and they, also, felt he was alcoholic and were concerned. He yelled at her for involving his family. She pointed out they were her family as well and that they all loved him and wanted him to stay alive. He said he would do whatever he wanted, whenever he wanted, and started out the door. She told him, very quietly, that if he left for a bar now, the locks would be changed when he got back and she would start divorce proceedings in the morning. He laughed and walked out.

Once again, Carole called Tom. He reassured her that she

had done the right thing and helped her find the number of an all-night locksmith. Tom and his wife came over to the house, and after paying an exorbitant sum to have the front and back door locks changed, decided to stay with Carole and await Jonathan's return.

Jonathan, meanwhile, had headed straight for the nearest bar, furious with the world for treating him so badly and with Carole for betraying his trust. After several drinks he decided to call his mother and ask if he could stay with her for a few days. His mother, aware of the situation, refused, telling him to get treatment. He called each of his brothers in turn and got the same answer. He called his best friend, who had already heard from Carole, and was told that not only would he not allow Jonathan to stay in his home, but also that he did not want to hear from Jonathan again until Jonathan was in a treatment hospital.

Jonathan was now precariously balanced between blind rage and tears. He slammed the phone down so hard that the receiver cracked and the cradle snapped off. The bartender angrily asked him what the hell he thought he was doing and motioned to the bouncer to remove Jonathan from the bar. Blind rage won.

Jonathan swung at the massive bulk of the bouncer, missing by a mile. The bouncer, well trained in dealing with drunken customers, put Jonathan in a headlock and propelled him out the door. Jonathan was now completely out of control, and came barreling back into the bar, knocking over a table and some chairs as he ran at the bouncer.

By the time it was all over the police had been called, the

bouncer had bruised knuckles, and Jonathan was under arrest—with a black eye.

Carole got the call at about 1 A.M., and was about to rush down to the precinct when Tom stopped her and took the phone away.

"Jon? This is Tom. I'm not letting Carole go down there to get you until you promise to get into the hospital to take care of your alcoholism."

Jonathan exploded at his brother, accusing him of everything from interfering in his marriage to stealing his teddy bear when they were children. Tom listened for a while and handed the phone back to Carole, saying "It's got to come from you. Make him make a choice."

Carole, near tears herself, told Jonathan that she would not get him unless he promised to go in for treatment. Jonathan told her to go to hell and hung up.

It was a horrible night for Carole, but a worse one for Jonathan. He convinced the police to let him make two more calls, but in both cases Carole had reached them first. No one would come bail him out, even though the fine was low and the charge minor. He spent a long night in a holding cell, racked with tremors and aching from the fight. The next morning, thoroughly defeated, he persuaded the police to let him call Carole again.

It was a very different phone call. Jonathan begged Carole to come and get him, promised to go into treatment that very day if only she would take him back and stand by him.

Carole took him at his word. She called my office and told me that she was bringing Jonathan in, packed a bag with his clothes, and drove to the police station. It was the first step on the long road to recovery.

I will continue the story of Jonathan and his family over the next several chapters. Although Jonathan's degeneration and crisis occurred at a very rapid rate, his story is not unusual. He was lucky, however, in that he had a wife who both loved him and was smart enough to go for help herself, and a brother who had a real understanding of the disease and knew how to handle an active alcoholic. Far too many alcoholics never receive the intervention and treatment they desperately need.

CASE STUDY:
"Hunting with a Cat"

James M. was a highly successful insurance broker, aged fifty. An acknowledged success both financially and socially, he enjoyed an affluent life with his wife and children. Approximately five years before he came to see me, however, James had begun to experience physical symptoms that had become so disturbing he was considering an early retirement.

Three to four times a week, James experienced an odd tightening sensation in his head that was followed by a debilitating and prolonged headache. In addition, he was having difficulty remembering basic information and was extremely fatigued. He also reported vague numbness and tingling in his arms and legs.

These apparently neurological symptoms were accompanied by severe allergic rhinitis, particularly in the spring and fall, and frequent postnasal drip. His heart periodically raced and skipped beats, and he had frequent severe heartburn and indigestion.

During the past five years, James's weight had jumped from 175 pounds to 205 pounds, despite repeated attempts at a variety of diets, including liquid protein programs. His diet, as reported, was relatively balanced, although he did have frequent overwhelming cravings for sweets.

Before coming to me, James had seen an internist, a rheumatologist, a neurologist, a dentist (to rule out temporal mandibular joint syndrome), a chiropractor and spent a week at the Mayo Clinic. None of these physicians had been able to pinpoint the cause of his problems.

James's medical history was not remarkable. He was nearsighted, had a benign heart condition called lower right bundle branch, and in youth had an episode of what sounded like infectious mononucleosis. He had had mumps at age thirty-five, but had suffered no complications. Although he reported a certain sensitivity to chemical fumes such as tar, automobile exhaust fumes, and gas, nothing about his home or work environment appeared to contribute to his symptoms.

James indicated that his father had died of alcoholism, but was quick to discount any alcohol problem in his own case. His rather abrupt dismissal of the subject struck me as odd, given his willingness to give explicit details about every other aspect of his history and symptoms. I probed further, asking specifics about his drinking pattern. Although he admitted that his life might be better without drinking, he denied having any problem with drinking or suffering adverse effects as a result of drinking. He bridled a bit when I asked about prescription or illegal drug use, and I reminded him that alcohol was also a drug and his attitude about alcohol seemed quite different. He laughed and agreed.

Although James's blood pressure was elevated (a condition he laughingly attributed to "doctoritis") and his neck muscles rather tense, the initial physical exam revealed nothing significant. His lab results, on the other hand, were very revealing.

Although James was not anemic, his red blood cells were swollen and dysfunctional and his liver enzymes were elevated—two significant indications of alcoholism and early liver disease. Additional tests indicated that James's alcoholism had begun to affect his bone marrow and production of white blood cells, which were well below the normal range. His lipid metabolism was quite skewed, with a markedly elevated levels of serum triglycerides, all of which placed him at high risk for atherosclerotic disorders, heart attack, and stroke.

James's allergy tests showed he had considerable sensitivity to environmental antigens, particularly house dust mites and molds. He displayed adverse allergic reactions to corn, wheat, yeast, and coffee. As we know, corn, wheat, and yeast are all primary ingredients in most alcoholic beverages. When we put James on a diet free of corn, wheat, and yeast for four days he reported feeling considerably better. When we then gave him doses of wheat and corn we were able to induce the headaches he had been suffering from for five years.

Despite his lab results, James was strongly in denial of his alcoholism. He was, however, intrigued and excited by the allergy angle and quite willing to go on an allergen-free diet with nutritional supplementation in conjunction with regular office visits. Since it was obvious that this man would never consent to go into the hospital, we opted for a less direct method of detoxification.

There is a saying in Brazil, "If you don't have a dog, hunt with a cat." In James's case, the "cat" was his allergies.

Since James was so allergic to the components of alcoholic beverages, we added alcohol to the list of foods that he would have to cease consuming. In order to monitor any signs of withdrawal, we had him come in for daily checkups for the first week or so of his "allergy program."

On the second day James's blood pressure and pulse were up, and he was rather uncomfortable and irritable. I precribed a very low dosage of a benzodiazepine for five days in order to guard against seizures, telling him it was to help counteract the feelings of withdrawal he was experiencing as his body got used to the absence of alcohol, wheat, corn, yeast, etc.

Although James continued to improve on this regimen, he was still unwilling to accept that his primary problem—which was at the root of all his other disorders—was alcoholism. James was convinced that, although his father was alcoholic, he was different—"stronger"—than his father.

I felt that the laboratory evidence of liver disease, bone marrow toxicity, lipid malfunctions, and cardiovascular disease would be sufficient hard evidence to convince James of his alcoholism. I presented this information to James, explaining the link between genetics (his father's alcoholism) and his own situation, and the risks of letting it go uncorrected.

James at first became angry, hotly denying the connection and coming up with alternative reasons for his condition. We went back and forth for quite some time, with me reiterating that this was not a judgment of any kind, but simply a medical diagnosis, and that he now had an opportunity to get well and start a new healthy life instead of feeling over-the-hill and unwell, and retiring at fifty.

James finally agreed to stop drinking for three months, while continuing with his nutritional and exercise program. He also agreed to discontinue an anti-inflammatory drug that had been prescribed by another doctor, which placed him at risk for gastrointestinal bleeding, since the drug depressed blood clotting and James was already suffering from severe alcoholic gastritis.

Although he would not agree to stop drinking forever, he did not object when we went over the findings and their implications with his wife.

At the end of three months, James was without symptoms and feeling much better. He had lost weight, was feeling alert and full of energy, and no longer had headaches. Throughout this time my staff and I had tried to educate James and his family about the real nature of his alcoholism, and as James's condition improved he became much more accepting. Despite strong encouragement, however, he remained resistant to going to AA.

James M. has been in this state for two years now. His career and marriage are both doing well, and he has begun to make active efforts to teach his children about alcoholism. He has expressed a desire to keep them (as they enter their teens) from falling into the same trap that caught his father and himself. James still does not entirely believe that he can never drink again—and this is a dangerous belief that may yet trip him up—but he has come far, and we will continue to do what we can to support him and keep him well.

12

CHOOSING A TREATMENT PROGRAM

Even before you set out to convince your loved one to get treatment for his or her alcoholism, you must decide where that treatment is to take place. As I noted earlier, there are a large number of programs that claim (and genuinely believe) they are providing comprehensive treatment for alcoholism when they are actually neglecting the central biological nature of the disease.

This is why it is crucial that you be an informed consumer in investigating and choosing a treatment program.[1] Find one that offers complete biological restoration, not just a few days of detoxification, with detailed diagnostic testing, nutritional supplementation and retraining, immunological and neurological restoration, and an individually tailored exercise program. Be sure that in addition to individual and group counseling, the program offers some sort of behavioral training (such as role-playing) to help the alcoholic learn new ways to handle situations in which he or she used to drink. And be certain that the program is capable of involving you, your children, and other family members in the treatment process.

Whenever one is comparison shopping, it is important to know exactly what you want. When shopping for a good alcoholism treatment program, there are specific components that should be thoroughly investigated.

To do this, you must not be afraid to ask questions. Patients and their families are often frightened of making too many demands or asking too many questions of their physicians. They assume that doctor knows best and that they have no right to question his or her decisions or actions. Do not fall into this trap. When it comes to alcoholism, many doctors do not know best.

Communication and understanding are integral parts of alcoholism treatment. If the staff of a hospital or program is unwilling to talk to you and give you details on what the program entails, cross that hospital off your list. When doing your research, ask if there is a particular person whom you should talk to or a particular time that is most convenient. Make it clear that you are calling because you are considering bringing a patient in and you want to fully understand all aspects of the program before doing so. Talk to the admissions and billing offices to find out admission, insurance, and billing policies.

When questioning the staff members of any treatment program, there are several specific areas that you should particularly emphasize. The following sections are a basic checklist of the areas you should cover.

Diagnostic Testing

Treatment is only as good as the information on which it is based. In order to develop a truly comprehensive treatment plan, the doctors and staff must have a truly comprehensive knowledge of the patient's physical state. This requires careful laboratory testing and analysis, including:

- chest X ray
- full blood workup including:
    complete blood count
    protein metabolism
    lipid metabolism
    carbohydrate metabolism
    vitamin and mineral assays (if available)
    toxic metal screen
- complete urinalysis including:
    drug and alcohol screen
    evaluations for blood, bile, sugar, albumin, and acetone
    evaluations of pH and specific gravity
- EKG (within twenty-four hours of admission)
- Pap smear (for women, if not done within last year)
- allergen testing of blood sample (preferably using the RAST screening method). In persons with preexisting allergic symptoms such as asthma, chronic gastroenteritis, adverse food reactions, rashes, wheezing, or chronic fatigue, more detailed immunological evaluation, using skin test and other techniques, should be performed. Food, chemical, and environmental sensitivities should be thoroughly investigated

Any hospital that does not carry out at least these basic tests may not be paying sufficient attention to the biological complexity of alcoholism. In addition, any program that performs more than cursory psychological testing and diagnosis during the first five to ten days of recovery is in danger of making serious misdiagnoses. As we have seen, alcoholism causes drastic but temporary psychological and behavioral aberrations that can easily be mistaken for a primary psychiatric problem. While the facility must do a test of mental status to determine if the patient is a threat to himself, herself, or others, more detailed testing should be put off until after he or she has been stabilized. Such testing should occur after at least five days of detoxification, and preferably not until after three weeks of abstinence. In patients with severe alcoholism, results may still be skewed after up to three months of treatment.

SYSTEMIC TREATMENT

The facility should treat every patient as a distinct individual. Some patients require only short hospital stays and basic follow-up. Others require from three months to a year of inpatient treatment followed by very carefully supervised outpatient programs. The course of treatment should be defined by the specific biological and psychological needs of the patient as determined by the comprehensive testing outlined above.

In general, most patients should be medically detoxified and then go into an intensive three-week period of rehabilitation. This time period virtually guarantees that the patient will stay sober for at least a month and have a clear enough mind to be able to recognize and understand the nature of the disease. In addition, this ensures that the alcoholic will receive necessary nutrient supplementation and biochemical rehabilitation under close medical supervision.

The facility you select should be related to a medical institution with a trained nursing and medical staff, and it should have cardiac and intensive care units. This could be very important if the patient develops acute symptoms in these areas, either during detox or in subsequent treatment. If such care facilities are not actually on site, they should at least be readily available.

The actual treatment protocol should incorporate both the body and the mind—recognizing the genetic, metabolic, and nutritional components of the disease, as well as the psychobehavioral ones.

The alcoholic patient must literally learn a whole new way of life. From a medical perspective, *diet* is the cornerstone of effective rehabilitation. From a psychological perspective, major behavioral changes must be learned and reinforced. Crucial aspects of such a protocol include:

- dietary interventions—
    no refined sugar or carbohydrates
    no preservatives
    low salt
    fresh fruits, vegetables, and proteins
    healthy snacks between meals
    nonhydrogenated, low saturated fats
- nutritional supplementation—
    multivitamins

    amino acid supplements to help restore neurotransmitter
      balance

    specific nutrients as needed

- no drugs except in detox, if possible
- education—
    biology of alcoholism
    proper nutrition
- therapy—
    group
    individual
    family
    workshops and role-playing
- exercise facilities and programs
- a link with Alcoholics Anonymous, preferably with meetings on the ward during rehabilitation. Upon release, information should be provided on meetings in the patient's home or work areas. Each patient should be connected with a temporary sponsor while in the hospital, and this sponsor should accompany the patient to AA meetings after leaving the hospital

CONTINUING CARE OR AFTERCARE

The facility should maintain contact with the patient after leaving the hospital, through an established continuing care or aftercare program. Inpatient treatment is a lot like spring training—the real game does not start until the alcoholic is out in the world, facing the situations in which he or she used to drink.

Continuing care should provide the alcoholic with ongoing medical, psychological, and educational support. No patient should simply be released from the hospital and left to sink or swim on his or her own. In the first year or so of sobriety, the recovering alcoholic needs more than just AA meetings.

In particular, there should be a coordinated program of *medical* follow-up, complete with regular lab tests and urinalyses to monitor and encourage biological restoration. Nutritional changes and supplementation must be continued and encouraged to insure maximum recovery with maximum comfort. Regular visits with a physician trained in treating addictive diseases will ensure quick identification and treatment of any physical, nutritional, or immune system complications during recovery. This medical care should parallel continued involvement in education, counseling, and group programs.

This follow-up program should last for at least one year. Some programs use contracts with patients to ensure they understand the importance of continuing care. Others use contingency contracts in which the patient agrees to some sort of mild penalty for not complying with the follow-up (for instance, having to donate money to an organization he or she finds particularly offensive). The best way to ensure patient commitment is to involve the family and employer (if the employer knows of the person's alcoholism) in the program as well. Remember, the better the person with alcoholism feels physically, the less likely he or she is to return to drinking; and the surest way to optimize his or her health is to keep care going for at least a year.

OUTPATIENT OPTIONS

Since we do not live in the best of all possible worlds, there will be times when it will not be possible to get the alcoholic into a hospital. In these cases, it is still possible to follow the principles of care outlined in this chapter, as well as those in chapters 13 and 16. Whatever course you take, it is important to be in contact with and under the care of a physician who is specifically trained in treating alcoholism and other addictive disorders. You can obtain information on such physicians in your area by writing to

THE AMERICAN SOCIETY OF ADDICTION MEDICINE
12 WEST 21 STREET
NEW YORK, NY, 10010.

Your local medical association can also provide information on physicians in your area, and AA is always a good source of information and referrals.

While there is much that you can do to optimize the health of the alcoholic—through good nutrition, vitamins, and other life-style changes—alcoholism is still a serious medical disorder that should be handled by a physician, both in and out of the hospital. Be certain that you have access to such a physician, even if it is not possible to get the alcoholic person into a hospital for inpatient treatment.

Let us return to the story of Jonathan, the aerospace engineer. On the day Jonathan's wife brought him in to the program of which I am medical director, Jonathan was a physical

EXAMPLES OF PROPER TREATMENT PROCEDURES

Problem	Response
withdrawal	careful, medically supervised detoxification
malnutrition	intravenous or intramuscular nutrient replacement (five days), comprehensive multivitamins taken orally (day one through one year)
nutrient malabsorption	digestive enzyme supplements
abnormal carbohydrate metabolism	high protein, low-carbohydrate diet, avoidance of refined sugars, frequent small meals with healthy snacks between; comprehensive multivitamin supplements (lifelong change)
abnormal lipid metabolism	essential fatty acid supplements, natural, nonhydrogenated fats
mood disturbances or neurotransmitter imbalance	amino acid supplements
allergic responses to foods and environmental factors	allergy testing, rotation diet, desensitization if necessary
sleep disturbances	regular bed-time and wake-up schedules, reassurance that sleep regulation will return with time; tryptophan supplements if necessary
sexual dysfunction	reassurance, counseling, further testing if condition does not improve in first twelve months of sobriety
poor muscle tone or diminished stamina	supervised exercise program, based on cardiac and physical limitations
liver damage or hepatitis	all of the above
hypertension	all of the above; should vanish as treatment progresses, should be reevaluated over time

**EXAMPLES OF PROPER TREATMENT
PROCEDURES**

Problem	Response
memory loss, mental clouding, etc.	all of above, after possible head injuries have been ruled out
impaired family relationships	group and individual counseling
denial	all of above, plus intensive education

wreck. He was twenty-five pounds overweight and looked bloated and pale. His eyes (one still bruised from the bar fight) were bloodshot; and his gaze darted around the room. His blood pressure was markedly elevated, his pulse rapid, and fine tremors shook his hands. He complained of pain in his side and an inability to sleep, and began a rambling discourse on the problem he had had at work that had caused his drinking.

I explained that his pain and insomnia were the result of his body withdrawing from alcohol, and that the detoxification protocol would relieve his discomfort. The nature of the protocol was carefully laid out, and I explained to Jonathan that we would be medicating him for a short time. This medication was to relieve the effects of withdrawal on the cells of the brain that had been disrupted by alcohol and its by-products, and would be discontinued when the crisis stage of withdrawal was past.

Although I am strongly against the unnecessary use of addictive drugs during alcoholism treatment, in the early stages of detoxification the prime objective is to keep the patient comfortable and minimize potentially fatal withdrawal symptoms such as seizures, or complications such as heart attack or stroke. Research is being done on how to detoxify alcoholics without drugs, but until such methods are developed no patient should be made to tough it out through withdrawal. Medication—either phenobarbital or one of the benzodiaze-pines—is appropriate during early detoxification and should be discontinued as soon as possible.

I strongly emphasized that Jonathan had to work *with* the treatment staff as part of a team in order to detoxify him with as little distress as possible. He was cautioned to notify the staff on the unit if any alarming symptoms arose or if he felt his discomfort was too severe to handle.

After the initial physical exam—during which I ordered blood and urine samples for more detailed analysis as well as a skull X ray to check for any undetected injuries from the fight—Jonathan was placed on fifty milligrams of Librium, to be repeated every four hours. If Jonathan's distress became acute, the staff was instructed to give him an additional fifty milligrams every two to three hours, in between doses. This dosage was reduced gradually over the next four days.

Jonathan was also given an intramuscular injection of a mul-tivitamin supplement and placed on a schedule of regular mul-tivitamin supplementation by mouth. He was shown to his room, and shortly afterward fell into a deep sleep.

Carole, meanwhile, met with the social services staff to dis-cuss a schedule of weekly meetings between the treatment team, Jonathan, the children, and herself. She was told that Jonathan's progress would be quicker if she participated in the program and learned more about the disease and its conse-quences. Although Carole was at first reluctant to involve the children, she agreed when the counselor reminded her that the children had already been affected by Jonathan's alcoholism and would only be helped by learning what was wrong with their father.

Jonathan was examined again the next morning. His blood pressure was still high and his pulse still rapid, despite rather heavy sedation during the past eighteen hours. However, he appeared less anxious than he had the day before and seemed to trust that the staff was truly doing its best to ease his suffering.

Despite his elevated pulse and blood pressure, Jonathan was showing none of the other signs of impending D.T.'s or other severe complications of withdrawal. Conversation with him revealed that his thinking was still confused and distorted; he spoke disjointedly of needing to get back to work and feed the dog.

At the end of his first day, Jonathan's thought processes became less haphazard, and he told staff members that he was feeling extremely depressed and despairing. While this was not unexpected (90 percent of alcoholic patients exhibit depression), the staff kept a close watch in case he should start developing thoughts of suicide.

By the third day, Jonathan was down to a markedly decreased level of Librium and by the end of the fourth day the Librium was discontinued. At this point, Jonathan was also beginning to feel considerably better, both physically and mentally. His depression, though still present, had lifted somewhat, and his thinking had become clearer.

On the fourth day of Jonathan's detoxification I recommended that he go into a rehabilitation program for twenty-eight days. Jonathan's denial quickly rose to the surface. He could not stay because his funds were running out and he had no job. His family needed him. His dog only ate a certain kind of dog food and only he, Jonathan, know where to buy it and how to serve it. Twenty-eight days was out of the question. The team, consisting of the social worker, the nurse, and myself, countered all these objections by explaining to him *that he was just beginning to recover and that his alcoholism must be his first priority.* We explained that he was barely out of the woods, medically, and that his family did not need him back if he was not entirely well.

Jonathan said he would think about it for a while.

That same day we held another meeting with Jonathan, his wife, and the treatment team. While the treatment team reiterated the earlier arguments, Carole firmly informed Jonathan that if he was not willing to fully commit to getting well she did not want him back. She wanted a sober, healthy husband, not a "dried-up drunk" or an active alcoholic. She was willing to endure financial hardship and stand by him only as long as he was willing to make a true commitment to combating his disease. Nothing else was acceptable.

Jonathan agreed to further treatment, and on the fifth day of detoxification was transferred to the rehabilitation unit. The first stage was over.

At that point, Jonathan was out of immediate physical trouble, and was sent to the AA meetings which occur nightly in our wards. Initially he was reluctant to attend these meetings, since he felt that AA was for losers or religious fanatics. We dispelled these misconceptions, explaining that the AA step process was crucial to learning to live without alcohol and that

AA had pioneered and understood the disease model of alcohol some thirty years before the medical establishment caught on. Finally, we stressed that AA was an integral part of our rehabilitation program, and that while he was at this facility he must go to AA meetings.

At the same time, Jonathan attended a variety of classes on the biology of alcoholism and the importance of proper nutrition in maintaining serene sobriety. He responded well, as he began to realize that his alcoholism was indeed a disease and not some moral weakness.

Jonathan began a program of psychological counseling that included individual and family meetings, as well as extensive group sessions. Jonathan did particularly well in the role-playing exercises and showed a great talent for imagining situations in which it would be difficult to resist drinking. As time went by he became equally adept at coming up with alternative behaviors.

Jonathan was particularly anxious about his lack of sexual desire and impotence, and expressed concern that this condition would be permanent. Counselors and teachers alike reassured him that the sexual dysfunctions he had experienced were a common symptom in alcoholism and that normal sexual function would return as his body recovered.

Major emphasis was placed on nutrition. Throughout rehab, Jonathan was given a broad spectrum nutrient supplement as well as calcium and phosphorus and a gram of ascorbic acid daily. The foods which were giving him the greatest trouble in terms of adverse reactions were removed from his diet. He was put on a regimen of green vegetables, fresh fruits, and protein.

Jonathan, like so many other patients with alcoholism, demonstrated adverse reactions to molds, wheat, corn, and potatoes—the *major ingredients* of many alcoholic beverages. Jonathan was also detoxified during this period from caffeine, sugar, food additives, chemicals, and junk foods.

His weight began to change very markedly; he went through a period of diuresis. The dietitian worked carefully with him and his wife, explaining the necessity of eating a greater variety of whole foods at frequent small meals. She helped develop a rotational diet for Jonathan, based on the foods to which he was allergic, that would minimize his allergic responses and reduce his cravings for certain foods—including alcohol.

At the end of the first ten days Jonathan was allowed to go outside to the gym. The activity director formulated a progressive program for him, based on instructions from the medical director, designed to get his endorphins and other neurotransmitters regulated again. Thus, the long path to bringing him back into shape was begun.

After twenty-eight days of rehab most of Jonathan's symptoms had vanished. He had lost twenty pounds, his body was beginning to firm up, and the bloat and pallor that had characterized him on admission had gone away. His energy was returning; his sleep pattern was approaching normal; and he was even beginning to experience some morning erections which signaled a returning sex drive. Lab tests revealed the early signs of liver disease that Jonathan had exhibited on admission were now resolving and that his nutritional status was greatly improved.

Jonathan was feeling much better psychologically as well. While he still suffered from bouts of anxiety—some of which had recognizable and justifiable causes—his depression had lifted almost entirely. The warm and engaging personality that Carole had first fallen in love with returned, and with it a reopening of communication between Jonathan and Carole. In fact, as Jonathan's family participated in treatment together, lines of communication reopened between all the family members. Accumulated pain, anger, and confusion were finally faced and dealt with, and many old wounds were reopened and healed. For the first time in several years, they began to knit together as a unit.

The restoration of his family had a remarkable effect on Jonathan. Despite his very understandable fears about leaving the hospital and finding a new job, Jonathan now felt assured that he had a secure and loving base with his wife and children.

In going over these results with Jonathan and Carole, I emphasized that these improvements would only last if Jonathan maintained the healthy life-style he was learning in the hospital. Upon release it was crucial that Jonathan continue to exercise, eat correctly, take vitamin supplements, and go to AA and aftercare. Only then could he be sure of continued mental and physical well-being.

That was how one alcoholism treatment program got one alcoholic patient sober. I will deal with how he was *kept* sober in the next chapter.

13

LONG-TERM RECOVERY— GETTING HIGH AND STAYING THAT WAY

There are a lot of people, alcoholics and nonalcoholics alike, who think a diagnosis of alcoholism is an irrevocable sentence to a life of deprivation. "Alcoholics can't have fun anymore." "Alcoholics only socialize with other alcoholics." "The life of the alcoholic is completely centered around AA."

These are absurd misconceptions, but they say a lot about our society and our attitudes toward drugs and alcohol. We have, as a nation, become remarkably dependent on outside agents for our sense of happiness and well-being.

What we as a society have forgotten, and what the alcoholic must learn, is that all the power we attribute to drugs and alcohol is actually in our bodies. The only reason alcohol and other drugs work is because they stimulate and accelerate the body's normal processes. For every high that a drug produces, there is a natural biological equivalent that will feel better, last longer, and have no unpleasant side effects.

Because of this, alcoholism can actually be a great liberator for those with the disease. Alcoholism, like diabetes, sets its own limits—on diet, on behavior, on every aspect of the alcoholic's life-style. At the same time, it opens a door to a world of new health and vitality that most Americans never experience. Alcoholism may be the only disease of our time that can literally give its victims a new and better lease on life.

The terms of this lease are very clear and explicit, and once the alcoholic has finished the initial stages of treatment he or she must accept these terms for life.

Alcoholics can no more change their alcoholism than they can change their fingerprints—it is genetically encoded into the very cells of their bodies. And once alcoholism has been established it will not go away. Detoxification and rehabilitation will not miraculously restore the body to its predrinking state.

If an alcoholic drinks—no matter how long he or she has been sober—he or she will not only resume drinking, but also will actually *exceed* the amounts he or she used to consume. This phenomenon—known clinically as *progression*—is a result of alcoholism's permanent effects on the liver and other organs that process nutrients and toxins. No matter how long the alcoholic abstains, these metabolic effects remain in place, waiting to be triggered by alcohol.[1]

These same metabolic changes also make the alcoholic far more susceptible to the effects of other drugs. It is for this reason that the alcoholic must be taught to avoid drugs of any kind. All too often, alcoholics recover from alcohol addiction only to become addicted to some other drug. Alcoholics in recovery must abstain from *all psychoactive substances,* from scotch to caffeine and over-the-counter cold medicines—if they wish to experience truly "serene sobriety." Alcoholics need to be very informed consumers and watch out for alcohol that may be present in seemingly innocuous foods and medications.

The following listings will help the person with alcoholism choose safe medications and avoid risky ones. To provide a basis for comparison, look at the alcohol content of some of the most common alcoholic beverages:

beer and malt liquor	3.6 to 6.3 percent
bourbon	40 to 57 percent
gin	47 percent
rum	43 to 75.5 percent
scotch	43 percent
vodka	45 to 50 percent
wine	11 to 14 percent

On a purely percentage level, many of the medications listed below[2] have a higher concentration of alcohol than a bottle of beer.

One of Alcoholics Anonymous' most useful axioms is expressed by the acronym *HALT*—never get Hungry, Angry, Lonely, or Tired. This simple instruction shows a great understanding of the nature of alcoholism and the needs of alcoholics. Let's examine each point.

H—Hunger. As you know, alcoholism causes systemic malnutrition with severe alterations in blood glucose levels and neurotransmitter production. When alcoholics skip meals or eat snacks high in sugar and refined carbohydrates, their glucose levels rise and fall dramatically. These peaks and valleys can cause severe mood swings, so it is important that alcoholics eat well and often so that their brains get a steady supply of glucose. Protein foods (such as cheese and nuts) and complex carbohydrates (such as fruits and vegetables) are good between

Item	Use	Manufacturer	Percent Alcohol Content
Ambenyl	cough suppressant	Forest Pharm.	5
Ambenyl-D	expectorant, nasal decongestant, cough suppressant	Forest Pharm.	9.5
Anbesol	oral antiseptic, anesthetic	Whitehall Labs.	70
Asbron G Elixir	antiasthmatic	Sandoz Pharm.	15
Bayer Children's Cough Syrup	cough suppressant, nasal decongestant	Glenbrook Labs.	5
Benadryl Decongestant Elixir	antihistamine	Parke-Davis	5
Benadryl Elixir	antihistamine	Parke-Davis	14
Benylin Cough Syrup	cough suppressant	Parke-Davis	5
Benylin DM	cough suppressant	Parke-Davis	5
Benylin Expectorant	cough suppressant, expectorant	Parke-Davis	5
Bronkolixir	bronchodilator, decongestant	Winthrop Pharm.	19
Cēpacol/Cēpacol Mint	mouthwash, gargle	Lakeslde Pharm.	14.5
Ce-Vi-Sol	vitamin C drops (for infants)	Mead Johnson Nutritionals	5
Cheracol D	cough suppressant, decongestant	Upjohn	4.75
Cheracol Plus	cough suppressant, decongestant	Upjohn	8
Chlor-Trimeton Allergy Syrup	antihistamine	Schering	7
Choledyl Elixir	bronchodilator	Parke-Davis	20
Colace Syrup	laxative	Mead Johnson Pharm.	1
Colgate Mouthwash	mouthwash	Colgate-Palmolive	15.3
CONTAC Nightime Cold Medicine	antihistamine, analgesic, cough suppressant, decongestant	SmithKline	25

Item	Use	Manufacturer	Percent Alcohol Content
Dilaudid Cough Syrup	cough suppressant, analgesic	Knoll	5
Dimetane Elixir	antihistamine	Robins	3
Dimetane Decongestant Elixir	antihistamine, decongestant	Robins	2.3
Dimetapp Elixir	decongestant, antihistamine	Robins	2.3
Diuril Oral Suspension	diuretic, antihypertensive	Merck Sharp & Dohme	0.5
Donnatal Elixir	antispasmodic	Robins	23
Elixophyllin-KI Elixir	antiasthmatic	Forest Pharm.	10
Feosol Elixir	iron supplement	SmithKline	5
Fergon Elixir	iron supplement	Winthrop	7
Geriplex-FS Liquid	vitamins (geriatric)	Parke-Davis	18
Geritol Liquid	vitamins	Beecham	12
Geritonic Liquid	vitamins	Geriatric Pharm. Corp.	20
Gevrabon	vitamins	Lederle	18
Hycotuss	expectorant	DuPont	10
I.L.X. B_{12} Elixir	iron supplement	Kenwood	8
Iberet-Liquid	vitamins	Abbott	1
Imodium A-D	antidiarrheal	McNeil	5.25
Incremin	vitamins	Lederle	0.75
Indocin Oral Suspension	analgesic	Merck Sharp & Dohme	1
Kaochlor S-F	potassium supplement	Adria	5
Kaon-Cl 20% Liquid	potassium and chloride supplement	Adria	5
Kaon Elixir	potassium supplement	Adria	5
Kay Ciel Oral Solution	potassium supplement	Forest Pharm.	4
Klorvess 10% Liquid	potassium and chloride supplement	Sandoz Pharm.	0.75
Lanoxin Elixir Pediatric	cardiac medication	Burroughs Wellcome	10
Lasix Oral Solution	diuretic	Hoechst-Roussel	11.5

Item	Use	Manufacturer	Percent Alcohol Content
Listerine Antiseptic	mouthwash/gargle	Warner-Lambert	26.9
Lomotil Liquid	antidiarrheal	G.D. Searle & Co.	15
Lufyllin Elixir	bronchodilator	Wallace	20
Marax DF Syrup	bronchodilator	Roerig	5
May-Vita Elixir	vitamins	Mayrand	13
Mediatric Liquid	estrogen replacement	Wyeth-Ayerst	15
Mellaril Oral Solution	antipsychotic	Sandoz Pharm.	3 to 4.2
Mestinon Syrup	treatment of myasthenia gravis	Roche Labs.	5
Naldecon DX Pediatric Drops	decongestant	Bristol Labs.	0.6
Naldecon DX Children's Syrup	decongestant, cough suppressant, expectorant	Bristol Labs.	5
Nicotinex Elixir	niacin supplement	Fleming	14
Niferex Elixir	iron supplement	Central Pharm.	10
Novahistine Elixir	antihistamine, decongestant	Lakeside Pharm.	5
Novahistine Expectorant	cough suppressant, decongestant, expectorant	Lakeside Pharm.	7.5
Nucofed Expectorant	cough suppressant, decongestant, expectorant	Beecham Labs.	12.5
Nucofed Pediatric Expectorant	cough suppressant, decongestant, expectorant	Beecham Labs.	6
Nu-Iron Elixir	iron supplement	Mayrand	10
Nystex Oral Suspension	antifungal antibiotic	Savage	1
Organidin Elixir	expectorant	Wallace	21.75
PBZ Elixir	antihistamine	Geigy	12
Pamelor Solution	antidepressant	Sandoz Pharm.	3 to 5
Peri-Colace Syrup	laxative	Mead Johnson Pharm.	10
Permitil Oral Concentrate	antipsychotic	Schering	1

Item	Use	Manufacturer	Percent Alcohol Content
Phenergan Syrup Fortis	antihistamine	Wyeth-Ayerst	1.5
Phenergan Syrup Plain	antihistamine	Wyeth-Ayerst	7
Phenobarbital Elixir	sedative	Roxane	13.5
Polaramine Syrup	antihistamine	Schering	6
Poly-Histine Elixir	cough suppressant	Bock	4
Prolixin Elixir	antipsychotic	Princeton	14
Quelidrine Syrup	cough suppressant	Abbott	2
Robitussin	expectorant	Robins	3.5
Robitussin A-C	cough suppressant, expectorant	Robins	3.5
Robitussin-CF	cough suppressant, decongestant, expectorant	Robins	3.5
Robitussin-DAC	expectorant, decongestant, cough suppressant	Robins	1.9
Robitussin Night Relief	analgesic, cough suppressant, decongestant	Robins	25
Robitussin-PE	decongestant, expectorant	Robins	1.4
Sandimmune Oral Solution	immunosuppressant	Sandoz Pharm.	12.5
Scot-Tussin Sugar-Free Expectorant	expectorant	Scot-Tussin	3.5
Sominex Liquid	sleep aid	Beecham Products	10
Sudafed Cough Syrup	decongestant	Burroughs Wellcome	2.4
Tacaryl Syrup	antihistamine	Westwood	7.37
Tagamet HCl Liquid	ulcer medication	Smith Kline French	2.8
Tavist Syrup	antihistamine	Sandoz Pharm.	5.5
Theo-Organidin Elixir	bronchodilator/expectorant	Wallace	15
Triaminic Expectorant	expectorant, decongestant	Sandoz Consumer Health	5
Tussar SF	cough suppressant	Rorer Pharm.	12
Tussar-2	cough suppressant	Rorer Pharm.	5

Item	Use	Manufacturer	Percent Alcohol Content
Tussend Expectorant	cough suppressant, decongestant, expectorant	Lakeside Pharm.	12.5
Tussend Liquid	cough suppressant	Lakeside Pharm.	5
Tylenol Adult Liquid Pain Reliever	analgesic	McNeil	7
Tylenol Cold Medication Liquid	analgesic, decongestant, cough suppressant, antihistamine	McNeil	7
Tylenol with Codeine Phosphate Elixir	analgesic	McNeil	7
Vicks Daycare Daytime Colds-Medicine Liquid	decongestant, analgesic, expectorant, cough suppressant	Richardson-Vicks	10
Vicks Formula 44 Cough Mixture	cough suppressant, antihistamine	Richardson-Vicks	10
Vicks Formula 44D Decongestant Cough Mixture	cough suppressant, decongestant	Richardson-Vicks	10
Vicks Formula 44M Multi-Symptom Cough Mixture	cough suppressant, decongestant, analgesic	Richardson-Vicks	20
Vicks Nyquil Nighttime Colds Medicine	decongestant, cough suppressant, antihistamine, analgesic	Richardson-Vicks	25

ALCOHOL-FREE MEDICATIONS

Item	Use	Manufacturer
Actifed Syrup	decongestant	Burroughs Wellcome
Bentyl Syrup	antispasmodic	Lakeside Pharma.
Chloraseptic Liquid	anesthetic and antiseptic mouthwash/gargle	Richardson-Vicks
Colace Liquid	laxative	Mead Johnson Pharm.
Gly-Oxide Liquid	oral anesthetic, anti-inflammatory	Marion Labs.
Haldol Concentrate	antipsychotic	McNeil
Kaopectate	antidiarrheal	Upjohn
Kwelcof Liquid	cough suppressant	B.F. Ascher & Co.
Liquiprin Drops and Elixir	analgesic	Norcliff Thayer
Maalox Suspension	antacid	Rorer Pharm.
Mylanta Liquid	antacid, antigas	Stuart Pharm.
Mysoline Suspension	anticonvulsant	Wyeth-Ayerst Labs.
Naldecon CX Adult Liquid	cough suppressant, expectorant	Bristol Labs.
Naldecon DX Adult Liquid	decongestant, expectorant, cough suppressant	Bristol Labs.
Naldecon Senior EX Cough/Cold Liquid	expectorant	Bristol Labs.
Nucofed Syrup	cough suppressant, decongestant	Beecham Labs.
Pepto-Bismol	antacid, antigas, antidiarrheal	Procter & Gamble
Periactin Syrup	antihistamine	Merck Sharp & Dohme
Proventil Syrup	antiasthmatic	Schering
Scott-Tussin Sugar-Free DM Cough & Cold Medicine	cough suppressant, decongestant	Scot-Tussin
Sinequan Oral Concentrate	antidepressant	Roerig
Slo-Phyllin Syrup	antiasthmatic	Rorer Pharm.
Stelazine Concentrate	antianxiety, antipsychotic	Smith Kline & French
Sudafed Plus Liquid	decongestant, antihistamine	Burroughs Wellcome
Sumycin Syrup	antibiotic	Squibb
Theolair Liquid	antiasthmatic	3M Riker
Theolair-Plus Liquid	antiasthmatic	3M Riker

ALCOHOL-FREE MEDICATIONS

Item	Use	Manufacturer
Thorazine Syrup	antipsychotic	Smith Kline & French
Triaminic Cold Syrup	decongestant, antihistamine	Sandoz Consumer Health
Triaminic-DM Cough Formula	cough suppressant, decongestant	Sandoz Consumer Health
Triaminic Nite Light Nighttime Cough & Cold Medicine for Children	cough suppressant, decongestant	Sandoz Consumer Health
Triaminicol Multi-Symptom Cold Syrup	cough suppressant, decongestant	Sandoz Consumer Health
Tussirex Sugar-Free; Alcohol-Free, Dye-Free	cough suppressant	Scot-Tussin
Vicks Children's Cough Syrup	cough suppressant, expectorant	Richardson-Vicks
Vicks Children's Nyquil	cough suppressant, decongestant, antihistamine	Richardson-Vicks
Vistaril Oral Suspension	antianxiety	Pfizer

meal snacks, since the body breaks these foods down more slowly than simple carbohydrates, providing a more consistent flow of glucose to the brain.

Many alcoholics are allergic or sensitive to artificial preservatives, colors, and additives. When choosing foods, recovering alcoholics should stick to natural foods that have been grown and processed with a minimum of chemical additives. This means avoiding packaged foods and mix-with-water-and-serve meals, and particularly avoiding anything with a color that does not occur in nature—such as fluorescent purple blueberry pies or incandescent orange processed cheese foods. Later in the book I will provide a detailed nutritional program for the recovering alcoholic.

A—Anger. Impulsive and angry behavior is actually a side effect of becoming hungry. When the brain is being poorly fed natural neurotransmitter balances are distorted, leading to possibly violent mood swings and angry outbursts.

On a purely psychological-behavioral level, the stress of learning a new life without alcohol can cause some alcoholics to become angry and resentful and lead them into a vicious circle of unhealthy eating and life-style habits and continued mood swings.

L—Loneliness. Poor nutrition can also lead to bouts of depression in recovering alcoholics and a withdrawal from their families and support groups. Such withdrawal can be very dangerous, since in its worst manifestation it can lead to suicide or at least to renewed drinking. Lines of communication should always be kept open, and alcoholics should avoid becoming isolated from their sources of encouragement and support.

T—Tiredness. In general, whenever a person is tired he or she is more prone to make mistakes, have an accident, do something foolish or potentially destructive. This is also true of alcoholics.

The alcoholic can avoid becoming tired in a variety of ways. Good nutrition with a proper balance of protein, complex carbohydrates, and unsaturated fats will ensure a more steady supply of energy to every system of the body. Regular exercise (enough to work up a sweat) three or more times a week will also increase stamina and vigor, particularly if the activity is something the person really enjoys. And nutrient supplements, particularly of the amino acid precursors of natural neurotransmitters—such as glutamine, tryptophan, or L-tyrosine—will help the brain to recover normal production of the chemicals which provide the natural high of good health.

Alcoholism is a behavioral as well as biological disease, and behaviors are difficult to change even after the body has begun to be restored. Alcoholics have been well-conditioned to a life that centered around alcohol. When out of the controlled environment of the hospital or clinic, alcoholics must scrupulously avoid the places and people that in the past encouraged their addiction.

Alcoholics should not try to drink club soda at the bars where once they drank themselves into a stupor. Alcoholics should not spend time with and try to cure their friends who are actively drinking. If these friends try to convince the alcoholic that one little drink won't hurt, they should be avoided like the plague. Anyone who claims that an alcoholic can be a controlled drinker is a fool playing craps in a crocodile's mouth— and the stake is the life of the alcoholic.

As time goes on, alcoholics may find themselves facing a new pitfall—a superman syndrome of overestimating their capacities and setting unrealistically high goals for themselves. As they begin to look, feel, and function better, these individuals may decide to swear off every bad habit they every had, to redo the basement, to finally train the dog, to read *War and Peace*, and to make up for every bad thing they ever did. The impulse is admirable but dangerous. Alcoholism is a *chronic* disease. It takes time to recover, and setting impossibly high goals can put incredible stress—physical and mental—on the person in recovery.

Here we see the wisdom of AA's one-day-at-a-time philosophy—their almost Zen focus on dealing with the here and now and not making too many grand plans for the future. Every alcoholic needs AA, if only because of the reality base AA and its members provide. As long as the alcoholic does indeed take it one day at a time, setting attainable goals and taking good care of his or her health and well-being, recovery can be a steady, enjoyable, invigorating process.

The following behavioral guidelines can help the alcoholic in developing an alcohol-free social and day-to-day life.[3]

Get involved in Alcoholics Anonymous. The twelve steps and twelve traditions of AA are applicable to everyone, and actually delineate a clear path to self-realization and development. However, it is not always easy to make the transition to AA, and the following steps can be useful:

- Get a temporary sponsor before leaving the hospital.
- Go to your first meeting with that sponsor or some other AA member.
- Remember that AA groups, like their members, have distinct personalities; give yourself time to get to know the group, and try several if you are not quite comfortable with your first.
- Attend a minimum of ninety meetings in your first ninety days.
- Mix your AA meetings with open, closed discussion, and step meetings.
- When comfortable in an AA group, join that group.
- Be on the lookout for a strong sponsor unless, of course, you are happy with your temporary sponsor.

- Follow the suggestions of your contact person.
- Stick with and learn from the "winners" in the fellowship, those who are comfortable in their sobriety and have been sober for some time.
- Try to open up and share at meetings as much as possible and be as honest as possible about your fears and feelings.
- Don't jump steps; take it slowly and one step at a time.
- Renew the first three steps each morning.
- Keep AA literature around to read in your spare time.
- Start the day by reading the twenty-four-hour-a-day book.

Steer clear of people, places, and things that used to prompt your drinking. Don't try to prove how strong you are by going to a bar with your old drinking buddies and trying to drink only club soda. During the first year of recovery total avoidance is the best bet.

- Keep all liquor and mood-changing substances out of your home.
- Don't go into bars and liquor stores.
- At parties, make sure you have a glass of soda or juice in your hand to "fill the gap."
- Increase the time you spend with nondrinking friends.
- Avoid friends who are active alcoholics.

Put some structure in your life.

- Plan your day with regular sleep, waking, meal, and snack times and *stick to this schedule.*
- Schedule regular times for exercise.

- Schedule regular times to read, meditate, or otherwise relax.
- Make out a reasonable budget and arrange payment plans with any creditors (with the help of a professional, if necessary) and *stick to this budget.*
- Resume your professional and personal responsibilities *gradually:* don't try and take everything on at once.

Keep in touch with your feelings and needs.

- Take a daily inventory of your goals, fears, failings, and assets.
- Keep a journal of your attitudes and feelings.
- Allow yourself time to meditate or pray every day.
- Don't take on so many jobs or projects that you have no time for yourself.
- Try to use your sense of humor to keep things in perspective.
- Avoid resentment and self-pity.
- Deal with each day as it comes; do not brood on the past or worry overmuch about the future.
- Avoid envy and jealousy; be aware of what is positive in your own life—your sobriety is a great gift.
- Maintain communication with your sponsor and make use of all your supports.
- Continue with individual therapy to work through personal issues.

Start to repair your family relationships.

- Be sensitive to the feelings of those around you.
- Play all family relationships by ear and try to be the best

father, mother, sister, brother, wife, or husband that you can be.

- Keep lines of communication open with all family members.
- Spend time with each family member individually.
- Do some things with each of them that they would like to do.
- Be caring and consistent in your dealings with your children.
- Continue family therapy, if necessary.

Expand your repertoire of activities that don't involve alcohol.

- Read more books for pleasure.
- Take up bowling or golf or some other physical activity with nondrinking friends.
- Go to movies or the theater.
- Go to concerts.
- Get involved in community groups that interest you.

Don't overdo it. Even though you may feel like you can take on the world, give yourself time to get really secure and stable.

- Don't reactivate any old emotional entanglements until you've been sober for a year.
- Don't try to quit smoking cold turkey; instead, cut down gradually.
- Don't feel responsible for the feelings of everyone around you; you can be sympathetic without taking on the blame.
- Don't try to save your alcoholic friends until you yourself have been sober for at least a year.

Always remember that your sobriety is your first priority. Anything (or anyone) that threatens this should be avoided like the plague until you fully understand why that person, place, or thing makes you want to drink and have found a way to handle this effectively without alcohol.

The Twelve Steps[4]

1. We admitted we were powerless over alcohol—that our lives had become unmanageable.
2. We came to believe that a Power greater than ourselves could restore us to sanity.
3. We made a decision to turn our will and our lives over to the care of God *as we understand Him.*
4. We made a searching and fearless moral inventory of ourselves.
5. We admitted to God, to ourselves, and to another human being the exact nature of our wrongs.
6. We were entirely ready to have God remove all these defects from our character.
7. We humbly asked Him to remove our shortcomings.
8. We made a list of all persons we had harmed, and became willing to make amends to them all.
9. We made direct amends to such people wherever possible, except when to do so would injure them or others.
10. We continued to take personal inventory and when we were wrong promptly admitted it.
11. We sought through prayer and meditation to improve our conscious contact with God *as we understood Him,* praying only for knowledge of His will and the power to carry that out.
12. Having made a spiritual awakening as the result of these steps, we tried to carry this message to alcoholics and to practice these principles in all our affairs.

"Do not be discouraged. No one among us has been able to maintain perfect adherence to these principles. We are not saints. The point is that we are willing to grow along spiritual lines. The principles we have set down are guidelines to spiritual progress. We claim spiritual progress rather than spiritual perfection."
[From *Alcoholics Anonymous* (The Big Book), 1976, pp. 59–60]

The Twelve Traditions

1. Our common welfare should come first; personal recovery depends upon AA unity.
2. For our group purpose there is but one ultimate authority—a loving God as He may express Himself in our group conscience. Our leaders are but trusted servants; they do not govern.
3. The only requirement for AA membership is a desire to stop drinking.
4. Each group should be autonomous except in matters affecting other groups or AA as a whole.
5. Each group has but one primary purpose—to carry its message to the alcoholic who still suffers.
6. An AA group ought never endorse, finance, or lend the AA name to any related facility or outside enterprise, lest problems of money, property, or prestige divert us from our primary purpose.
7. Every AA group ought to be fully self-supporting, declining outside contributions.
8. Alcoholics Anonymous should remain forever nonprofessional, but our service centers may employ special workers.
9. AA, as such, ought never be organized, but we may create service boards or committees directly responsible to those they serve.
10. Alcoholics Anonymous has no opinion on outside issues; hence the AA name ought never be drawn into public controversy.
11. Our public relations policy is based on attraction rather than promotion; we need always maintain personal anonymity at the level of press, radio, and films.
12. Anonymity is the spiritual foundation of all our traditions, ever reminding us to place principles before personalities.

[From *Alcoholics Anonymous* (The Big Book), 1976, p. 564]

Medically, the alcoholic has a long way to go to get his or her body and brain operating at peak efficiency. The following points are a very basic guideline and will work best if done in conjunction with regular care from a physician trained in treating addictive disorders.

Stay away from alcohol and all addictive drugs.

- Make sure that your doctor, dentist, and pharmacist all know about your alcoholism and prescribe accordingly.
- Postpone elective surgery (such as dental work) until you have been sober for several months. If you must have surgery, try to limit the amount of postoperative painkillers that you take.

Dual Diagnoses

Alcoholics are no more prone to psychiatric disorders than the rest of the population, but in some instances alcoholism can coexist with a primary psychiatric disorder, such as manic-depression or even schizophrenia. In these cases, it is important to clear the brain of alcohol and repair the damage of alcoholism as much as possible before determining the treatment for the psychiatric problem. Remember, alcoholism will affect any psychological test outcome.

Persons with dual diagnoses require specialized treatment and should be carefully monitored. It is crucial that all medications be taken on schedule in the correct doses, and that medication levels be adjusted as the patient's condition changes.

Any psychotropic medications should be nonaddictive. For example, if a patient has severe depression that is not relieved after the alcoholism has been cleared, a nonaddictive medication (such as a tricyclic antidepressant) should be prescribed, not a highly addictive benzodiazepine tranquilizer.

Steer clear of sugar, corn syrup, and other refined carbohydrates. (See chapter 16 for details.)

Steer clear of preservatives and artificial colors and flavors. If it can only be produced in a lab, don't eat it.

Avoid caffeine. Caffeine's stimulant effects will only aggravate disordered carbohydrate metabolism and cause jitteriness and anxiety.

Eat lots of fresh fruits, vegetables, and proteins. (See chapter 16 for details.)

Avoid foods which cause adverse reactions. Cutting down on allergens will improve overall immune function.

Eat well and often. Several small meals will provide a more constant flow of fuel to the brain and keep you from getting listless or fatigued during the day.

Get moving.

- Exercise is essential to getting your endorphins (the brain's natural opiates) back to normal.
- Start slowly with something you enjoy and work your way up to an hour or so of aerobic exercise each day. Aerobic exercise is best for your heart and lungs, and is defined as any constant movement that gets your pulse and heart rate to a level of maximum efficiency. Walking, bicycling, and swimming are all good, safe aerobic exercises.

Don't overdo it.

- You're not in particularly good shape, so don't try to qualify for the Olympics when you're fresh out of the hospital.
- Start with exercises that don't put you under too much strain. It's probably best to avoid jogging or running for a while, since you may be more prone to shin splints.
- Always give yourself plenty of warm-up time so your muscles are really stretched and ready to go.

Get your rest.

- Put yourself on a regular bedtime and waking schedule.
- If you have trouble sleeping, don't stay up and watch television. Go to bed at the set time and read if you can't fall asleep.
- Get up at the same time each day regardless of how little you've slept.
- Don't nap during the day. Your sleep pattern will even itself out fairly quickly.

Take your vitamins. (See chapter 16 for details.)

Use natural remedies.

- If you really have trouble sleeping, try L-tryptophan, not Sominex.
- Use decaffeinated coffees and teas as well as medications which don't contain alcohol. Read labels and ask questions.

Clean up the rest of your act (but only when you're comfortably sober). There's no sense in recovering from alcoholism and then smoking yourself to death. Once you're feeling really healthy and serenely sober (it won't hurt to wait a year), work on quitting smoking as well.

Learn meditation and other relaxation techniques. There are many meditation, relaxation, and pain-control techniques that are taught by reliable, trained practitioners. You do not have to shave your head and wear saffron robes to meditate (although if you look good in yellow you might consider it).

Remember, alcoholism is forever. You may be feeling great, looking great, and acting great. You may have been sober for one, five, or twenty years but you still have the same liver and you still have the same genes. It may be tempting to have just one drink—but don't. When you were a child you learned that fire was hot and kept your fingers away from it from then on. Show the same common sense with alcohol.

I have seen thousands of patients go through this process of recovery and come back to me utterly amazed at how well they felt. As their bodies recovered from the ravages of alcoholism and began to function at peak efficiency, these men and women discovered new heights of physical well-being. One woman told me about attending a wedding at which many of the guests became sloppily drunk and wondering how she ever could have thought that drinking was fun. A man told me that he had never in his adult life actually seen a sunrise until he had gotten sober. A woman said that she had always believed she was frigid until she finally kicked a fifteen year alcohol and Valium habit and discovered what an orgasm was.

Each and every one of these patients truly believed that their lives would be utterly miserable without alcohol. They had been so sick for so long that they could not imagine any other life and had been so brainwashed by society's infatuation with alcohol that they could no longer fathom life without it. When they were finally free of their addiction, and physically and psychologically rehabilitated and restored, they were stunned to discover that life without alcohol is not only possible, but wonderful.

In the case of Jonathan, the adjustment to an alcohol-free life was relatively easy. His temporary AA sponsor helped him to become comfortable in a local AA group, and Jonathan continued in our aftercare program for a year after his release from the hospital. He was fortunate in having a family that understood his disease, and his wife's continued involvement in Al-Anon helped her deal with her residual feelings of anger and frustration.

Medically, Jonathan and his family showed an extraordinary willingness to make dietary and life-style changes. Jonathan came in for regular medical follow-ups, and Carole and their two daughters adopted the same nutritional habits as Jonathan, which made his adjustment much easier.

Today, five years after I first met him, Jonathan remains sober, stable, and physically well. He was rehired by his former employers a few months after leaving the hospital, thanks to his own willingness to admit his problem and an assurance from me and his counselor that he was indeed doing well and was still under our care. He eventually got his promotion, and is now enjoying considerable success. His children (who also feel physically better since adjusting their life-styles) are no longer afraid to bring their friends home. And Carole, who once thought she would have to leave Jonathan, remains active in Al-Anon and continues to enjoy her career as an art director.

CASE STUDY:
"I Got Sober for This?"

Bill H. was a thirty-nine-year-old man whose life had never been particularly easy. His mother's alcoholism had caused major disruptions in his family as he was growing up, and Bill had to fend for himself during much of his childhood. The situation was worsened by the fact that Bill had a great deal of trouble learning. Today we know that Bill suffers from dyslexia—a disability that makes it difficult to properly interpret the written word. When Bill was a child, however, all it meant was that he was unable to keep up with the other kids. He felt inadequate and frustrated, and perceived himself as stupid. His mother, deep in her own alcoholism, did nothing to contradict this or support him.

Bill coped with his problems by trying extra hard to please and studying long hours into the night. He succeeded in graduating from high school and eventually got a job as a maintenance person in a local hospital.

Bill discovered alcohol at age thirteen, when his first drink made him feel confident, charming, and not quite so stupid. His drinking continued over the next seventeen years, so that by age thirty he had overt alcoholism. At thirty-seven he was drinking more than a fifth of alcohol a day and suffering from all the most dire physical consequences of alcoholism.

Bill, unlike many alcoholics, recognized the trouble he was in and went into a hospital to be detoxified. When he was released he felt a tremendous sense of pride and accomplishment and resolved to live his life to the fullest, without alcohol. He went to AA meetings regularly, doing the requisite "ninety meetings in ninety days," got a sponsor, and never had another drink.

And he felt simply awful for two full years.

Not long after he got out of the hospital, Bill started having episodes of dizziness and disorientation. On two occasions he actually fainted. He began to be chronically fatigued, and his energy level dropped dramatically. After several months of this, Bill began to feel terribly depressed, and on one occasion attempted suicide. Several doctors performed neurological workups on Bill but were unable to find a reason for his symptoms.

Bill also found that he was craving alcohol, so he followed the AA advice to have a candy bar or cup of coffee to cut down on alcohol cravings. By the time he came to my office (two years after he had been detoxified), Bill was drinking twenty cups of coffee a day and living almost entirely on candy, cakes, and cookies. He kept a supply of Snickers bars in his car, just in case.

When Bill was referred to me he was at the end of his rope. His fatigue and depression had become constant and so severe that he had been put on disability. He had chronic postnasal drip and stuffy nose. The neurologists and psychotherapists he had seen had done their best but had been unable to help him. When he came to my office his only comment was, "I got sober for this?"

A simple physical examination revealed nothing extraordinary. He was slightly overweight, but his blood pressure, pulse, and heart rate seemed well within normal range. But his symptoms of dizziness and disorientation made me suspicious, so I ordered a six-hour glucose tolerance test (GTT). In the GTT, the patient fasts for a while and is then given a loading dose of glucose. Blood is drawn every hour to monitor how the body is processing the glucose.

In Bill's case, it was clear from the start that something was radically off kilter. In the first hour his blood sugar shot way up, just as it does in diabetic patients, and his insulin levels showed that his pancreas was oversecreting insulin. This caused a severe *drop* in both blood glucose and insulin levels, and Bill became dizzy, faint, and anxious, with a severe craving for sugar. His adrenal glands were also hypersecreting, increasing his anxiety and panic. Bill's reaction to the GTT was so severe, in fact, that we discontinued it.

But we had the information we needed. Bill had a severe problem with his carbohydrate metabolism, which he had obviously had for quite some time. His body had a great deal of difficulty maintaining a stable supply of glucose to the brain. When Bill was drinking, alcohol served as a substitute fuel. Now that alcohol was gone, he was treating his severe drops in blood sugar with candy, cakes, and caffeine. These highly refined carbohydrates caused his glucose and insulin levels to rise and fall dramatically, and were the cause of his anxiety and fatigue.

Bill's allergy tests showed he had an amazing degree of sensitivity to a wide variety of environmental factors and adverse food reactions—particularly grass, trees, weeds, house dust mites, molds, coffee, corn, rye, wheat, sugar, and oats. Since most of Bill's diet consisted of precisely the foods he was allergic to, it was small wonder that he was feeling terrible.

I told Bill the results of these tests and explained what they meant. Although he had been sober for two years, Bill had never really recovered from his alcoholism. All the metabolic, nutritional, and immunological aspects of the disease had remained. I told him that if he really wanted to feel well, we would have to finish the process he began when he had stopped alcohol two years before.

We established a dietary plan for Bill—one which eliminated sugar, caffeine, and chemical additives, and rotated or eliminated the other foods to which he was sensitive. Bill was taught the basics of proper nutrition, and learned to eat several small, healthful meals throughout the day, rather than waiting until he was faint with hunger before eating or only eating three times a day. We also placed him on a broad-spectrum nutrient supplement to augment his diet. We instituted a program of immunotherapy for the environmental agents which caused some of his symptoms, and worked with him to develop a reasonable exercise plan which included bicycling to and from work (he had enjoyed bicycling since he was a child, but stopped when the fainting episodes began). And we encouraged him to continue to devote time to AA.

Being on disability had severely demoralized Bill, and although he was enthusiastic about his new health program and his renewed feeling of vitality, it was obvious that his self-esteem was still very low. Despite his obvious intelligence, charm, and marvelous people skills, Bill considered himself to be stupid and slow because of his reading problem. I was troubled by this, and made inquiries about programs for adults with dyslexia. One, an occupational therapy program, seemed good for Bill, and I recommended it to him. He joined the program, and soon went on to a career in sales, where his charm and skill with people and innate business sense served him well.

Today, Bill has been without symptoms and physically stable

for more than two years. He is the top salesman in a middle-sized company, and just received an award for his work (a two-week vacation in the Caribbean). He continues to come to my office for regular checkups, and continues active in AA. When he slips and starts eating badly and feeling unwell he is quick to get back on track.

This man had come to me with a preliminary diagnosis of primary depression, inadequate personality, and a personality disorder. He was already on disability, and the prognosis was that this would be permanent. What I saw, after testing, was a man with a severe disorder of carbohydrate metabolism, severe respiratory allergies, multiple adverse food reactions, dyslexia, and recovering alcoholism. My prognosis was good, provided prompt nutritional, immunological, and life-style changes were instituted.

Bill H. is a classic example of the dry drunk—the alcoholic who has kicked alcohol, but only by gritting his or her teeth and suffering through feeling lousy all the time. There is no reason to endure this type of misery when recovering from alcoholism.

14

PREVENTION— DON'T LET IT HAPPEN TO YOU

*"There is no cure for birth or death
except to enjoy the interval."*

—*George Santayana*

Learning to truly enjoy the interval is the most basic principle of prevention. Instead of turning to alcohol, drugs, or other quick cures, we should learn to make maximum use of our biological potential for feeling good—to seek out natural, rather than unnatural, highs.

In alcoholism, an ounce of prevention is worth far more than a pound of cure. The principles of alcoholism prevention will not only ward off the development of alcoholism, they will also improve overall health and well-being.

Prevention is particularly important if you are the child or grandchild of an alcoholic. Don't deceive yourself with assertions that "I'm stronger than my father was" or "It will be different with me." Alcoholism is not a matter of strength, it is a matter of genetics. Remember, in the person susceptible to alcoholism, metabolism is stronger than free will. Don't take unnecessary risks with your life.

If you were raised in an alcoholic household, you have probably learned one of the many unhealthy coping styles that were discussed in chapter 10. These life-style patterns can be crippling in their own right, even if you are not yourself an active drinker. Be aware of your emotional and psychological alcoholic inheritance and do not be afraid to seek out help.

The children of alcoholics learn very early that it is dangerous to trust, feel, or talk about one's feelings. As a result of this early learning, many children of alcoholics develop a pattern of behavior that has been called codependency—a life-style which grows out of a central lack of self-esteem and self-worth. Codependent individuals have so little trust in their own feelings, needs, abilities, and inherent worth that they become almost completely other directed, basing their sense of self on external approval and appreciation. Some core characteristics of codependency are:

- problems with intimacy—an inability to fully trust others and express feelings and needs
- fear and denial of anger
- fear of confrontation and conflict
- pervasive sense of shame and low self-image
- fear of abandonment
- a need to be in control of self and others
- a need to be needed, to always have someone to take care of and feel indispensable
- a compulsive need for the approval and praise of others

- anxiety about making decisions or changes
- a tendency to make black-and-white judgments

Involvement in a group such as Adult Children of Alcoholics can help change these patterns and reopen the door to free expression and trust. In chapter 17 I will provide information on several support organizations for alcoholics and their families.

The various organizations for children of alcoholics are invaluable resources, but they are not without flaws.

If you become involved in such a group, it is crucial that you do not lose sight of the *biological inheritance* of alcoholism. No amount of soul-searching or therapy will change the unique metabolism you have inherited.

If you are the child of an alcoholic and having emotional problems, remember to both avoid alcohol and follow the dietary and behavioral guidelines for the recovering alcoholic.

If you are the child of an alcoholic, the safest course is to abstain from alcohol completely. Failing that, alcohol use should be limited and controlled. Remember that drinking, for you, is not a harmless recreation but a risky endeavour. Treat alcohol with the respect it deserves. If you do choose to drink:

- Restrict your drinking to once every four days.
- Restrict your consumption to one and a half ounces of ninety proof alcohol per drinking episode. (For a review of the alcohol content of various beverages, refer to chapter 13.)

In today's society it is often difficult to maintain such a moderate drinking pattern. Friends may encourage you to have just one more, others may be threatened by your self-control and attempt to embarrass you into heavier drinking. In these instances it is important to remember that alcoholism is not a social stigma, but a disease to which you may be highly susceptible. It is unlikely that your friends would encourage you to have just one more drink of arsenic. You should not be embarrassed to explain the reason for your drinking restrictions.

Even if you are not the child of an alcoholic, you should learn to use alcohol in moderation and wisely. Alcohol is a powerful drug, even if it is legal. While it is relaxing and enjoyable in small doses, it can make you a serious danger to yourself and others when it is abused. The following guidelines[1] should be observed when using alcohol:

- Don't drink alone.
- Never drink and drive.
- Never drink and operate machinery.
- Never mix alcohol and other drugs (including over-the-counter medications).
- Try not to drink on an empty stomach.
- Limit consumption to no more than 1 ½ ounces of ninety proof alcohol in a twenty-four-hour period.
- When you do drink too much, take plenty of nonalcoholic fluids to offset dehydration.
- Try not to drink every day.

Ultimately, you can decrease your risk of developing alcoholism by increasing your overall health. The principles of diet, exercise, and life-style which are outlined throughout this book—particularly in chapters 13 and 16—are applicable to everyone.

The most fundamental principle of good health is to take an active responsibility for your health. Don't wait until you are already sick to pay attention to your body's needs. Don't expect your doctor or pharmacist to miraculously cure years of physical abuse—whether from alcoholism, lack of exercise, poor nutrition, smoking, or all of the above. You are ultimately responsible for your own physical condition, and you have the power to activate your own natural highs. Do not blindly accept the empty promises of drug, alcohol, and food companies.

In medicine we have a saying, "When you hear hoofbeats, don't think of zebras." A similar principle may be applied to many aspects of modern life, "When you can't sleep, don't think of sleeping pills." "When you have a headache, don't think of aspirin." "When you feel anxious, don't think of tranquilizers."

Each of these conditions, from sleeplessness to anxiety, can often be cured by simply eating correctly and getting a proper balance of physical exercise and rest.

Our children are most susceptible to the seductive and illusory promises of modern manufacturers. Long-term prevention needs to start young. If you have children you need to make them aware of the dangers of alcohol and drug use at an early age, and you need to do far more than tell them to "just say no."

Human beings do not respond well to negatives. When told not to do something, most of us will either rebel outright or at least demand a damn good reason why. Children epitomize these responses. If you want your child to avoid alcohol and drugs, you'd better have some pretty good reasons and alternatives at your fingertips. And you'd better be setting a reasonable example of your own. Children are incredibly accurate barometers of hypocrisy. If you tell your son not to smoke marijuana while you finish a martini and light a cigarette, don't be surprised if he laughs in your face. The following guidelines are very basic.

Start them on a healthy life-style from infancy.

- Follow the nutritional principles from chapter 16.
- Encourage physical activity rather than hours of television. Make time for physical play with your children.

Teach them to think.

- Encourage your children to ask questions. When a particularly absurd commercial is on television, ask them whether they believe it and why. Teach your children never to accept things at face value, but to ask why something is being said or done and consider the motives of the person(s) involved.
- Encourage their individuality. Help your children learn not to conform. It will make it easier for them to resist peer pressure later in life.

Keep alcoholism and drug abuse out of the closet. Alcoholism and drug addictions are realities. Do not shroud them in mystery or moral posturing. Treat them as the diseases they are, and explain why they are dangerous.

Don't make alcohol and drugs attractive by making them symbols of rebellion or adulthood.

- Don't tell your children they cannot drink because they aren't grown up yet. Tell them that alcohol is powerful and dangerous and could hurt their bodies.
- Don't tell your children that drugs are evil and forbid their use. Explain the dangers of specific drugs, both physically and legally.

Give them the information to make informed decisions. Remember, there are plenty of people who make their livings telling kids that all the bad publicity about drugs is a lie. You have to give your children useful, noninflammatory information that will give them a good reason to "just say no."

Be there to listen when they need you. Growing up in today's society is a more complex affair than it was in days of yore. Although your children may seem sophisticated beyond their years, they are still children and need your support and supervision. Make some time to be with and talk to your kids every day, even if they don't seem to need it.

Current statistics indicate that at least one out of every three children aged fourteen through seventeen has experienced the negative consequences of using alcohol. The age of the first drinking experience is usually around twelve. Yet one out of every two parents is completely unaware of his or her child's drinking or drug use. Be on the lookout for the subtle signs of alcohol or drug use in your children before they have bloomed into full-blown alcoholism or drug addiction. Take particular note if your children evidence any of the following:

- drop in performance in school or at work:
  unexplained absences
  poor grades
  inability to complete projects or homework
  loss of interest in extracurricular activities, such as clubs or sports
- switch in peer group:
  abandonment or neglect of old friends
  attachment to new group
  unwillingness to introduce new friends to parents
- change in clothing and personal grooming:
  less attention to dress in formerly clothes-conscious person
  neglect of personal hygiene (bad breath, bathing less often, etc.)
  radical shift in clothing style
  tendency to wear long sleeves even on hot days (may indicate use of needles)
- increased tendency to isolate self from old friends and family
- decreased appetite and general disinterest in food

- frequent unexplained runny nose or bloodshot eyes
- sleep disturbances and/or sleepiness in school
- depression
- mood swings:
    increased aggression toward others
    agitation and nervousness
    listlessness and inappropriately "mellow" attitude
- when drinking is observed (particularly in those of legal drinking age), he or she cannot stop until dead drunk
- overt lying about drinking, with gross distortions of reality—"I only had one beer!"
- blackouts; these occur relatively early in the progression of problem drinking. If a young person cannot remember getting home from a party, be suspicious.

If you suspect alcohol or drug use in your child (or any young person), it is important that you address the problem as soon as possible. Angry accusations and confrontations can easily fuel an us-against-them mentality in young people who are caught up in the rebellious mystique of drug use. On the other hand, ignoring the situation or being timid about investigating what your child is doing can be equally destructive.

Friends are often aware of budding drug or alcohol problems, and may even wish to help but be restrained by a fear of being a snitch. If you are on good terms with your child's friends, you may wish to ask them about your child's drinking habits. Even if they are trying to cover for the problem drinker, a lot can be inferred from the way they respond to your questions. If they get nervous, will not meet your gaze, or try to uncomfortably laugh it off you can probably assume that some problem exists.

When dealing directly with your children, it is important to be direct, nonaccusatory, and firm in your concern. Even if you believe that drugs or alcohol are evil incarnate, it is probable that your child does not agree. Coming at this from a moral standpoint will only alienate your child further. Drugs and alcohol *are* physically and legally dangerous, however, and objections and concerns on these levels are not as easily debated. Even if your teenager thinks that marijuana should be legalized, the fact remains that it is not legal. Even if he thinks he can "hold" liquor well, the fact remains that high tolerance is a sign of incipient alcoholism. The basic facts of alcoholism and drug abuse are your strongest allies in interceding with children who may be making dangerous experiments with alcohol and drugs.

Ultimately, the most effective prevention of alcoholism and/or drug abuse is a firmly established healthy life-style (preferably starting in infancy) and solid, objective information about both the risks and the benefits of alcohol and other drugs of abuse. Adolescents will experiment with sex, cigarettes, alcohol, and many other things most parents would rather not think about. If they are enjoying the benefits of overall robust good health, however, unnatural and expensive highs will have less allure. And if they have been well educated in a noninflammatory, objective fashion of what drugs and alcohol actually *do*, they are far less likely to be seduced by the mystique of drug and alcohol use.

Interestingly, sometimes the most effective argument is neither medical nor moral, but economic—particularly when discussing illicit drugs. I have frequently asked younger audiences whether they would buy a steak from someone selling one from the backseat of a car. The response is usually a chorus of amused negatives. Why then, I ask, do so many people buy drugs that are made and sold by people they don't know, and which are sold at prices that exceed the gross national product of some Third World countries?

Most drugs sold on the street are cut with substances that are at best inert (like talc) and at worst deadly (like strychnine). Yet thousands upon thousands of young people who would never buy a pair of jeans without a designer label blindly believe pushers when they say some white powder is 99 percent pure cocaine. As one of my staff members (a veteran of much drug experimentation in the sixties) has put it, "There's no way in hell I'd do street drugs today. They could have been made anywhere by anybody. I've got better things to do with my nose than snort it full of talcum powder or lidocaine." (Lidocaine is a local anesthetic frequently mixed with talc to fool buyers into thinking they've bought cocaine.)

If all attempts at prevention fail, and your child does become involved in heavy alcohol or drug use, then a major intervention (using the principles outlined in chapter 11) is in order. The primary goal, superseding all others (including work, school, vacation, etc.) is to get your child alcohol and/or drug free. In these personal wars on drugs there should be no treaties or terms of surrender other than treatment and total abstinence.

The Big Picture

Prevention begins at home, but it should not stop there. We are facing a major health crisis in this nation, and most of our lawmakers, educators, and policymakers have absolutely no real understanding of the issues involved.

There is a very real possibility that in the near future it will be nearly impossible to get insurance coverage for alcoholism treatment and that research funding will be drastically cut. Alcoholism—the mother of almost all the other addictions—will be lost in the furor over the other drugs of abuse, and its toll on our nation's health and economy will continue to rise. There are steps that we, as individuals, can take to prevent this from happening. First, find out who your state and local legislators are and let your opinions be known.

- Demand that more funds be allotted for alcoholism research, treatment, and education.
- Press for the removal of all alcohol advertising from television.
- Request higher taxes on alcoholic beverages, and ask that this money be funneled into research, treatment, and education.
- Push for more insurance plans that cover comprehensive and long-term treatment for alcoholism.
- Protest unreasonable limitations on alcoholism treatment by insurance companies (also write to your union and the companies themselves).

On a local level, get involved in community and school groups to promote more awareness and understanding of alcoholism.

- Contact the National Council on Alcoholism for information on free educational programs.
- Get involved in your local chapters of Students Against Drunk Driving (SADD) or Mothers Against Drunk Driving (MADD).
- If none of these groups have chapters in your area, contact the national office and look into starting a chapter yourself.

We are all concerned about alcoholism and drug abuse in our society, but too few of us realize that we can have an impact. The success of groups such as MADD and SADD dramatically illustrate the power of grass-roots action on these issues. It really is possible to make a change.

CASE STUDY:
A Pharmaceutical Cornucopia

Jane R. was an attractive thirty-seven-year-old woman who was, on the face of it, living the suburban idyll. She was quite happy in her marriage, had no problems with her two children, and had a thriving free-lance career as an illustrator. She and her husband were more than financially comfortable and enjoyed an active social life.

Since the death of her father (three years prior to her visit), however, Jane had been suffering from severe bouts of depression and anxiety. She was also experiencing periods of disorientation and confusion.

At the time Jane came to my office, she was being maintained on several strong (and addictive) psychiatric medications. Foremost among these was Xanax, a benzodiazepine tranquilizer that is more potent than Valium. Her prescribed dosage was the equivalent of 100 milligrams of Valium a day, but she was also taking Valium when the Xanax failed to ease her anxiety, bringing her total dosage to more than 120 milligrams daily. She was also on Halcion—a sleeping pill that has many side effects including nerve damage, and Haldol—a potent antipsychotic drug that eases anxiety but also causes neurological damage over time. She was taking Fornate for her depression; HydroDiuril for her water retention and hypertension; and Benadryl for her frequent runny nose, skin rashes, and hives. In the past, she had also been on Elavil (an antidepressant), Ativan (another Valium relative), Navane (an antipsychotic), Mellaril (another antipsychotic), and Progentin (a drug to counteract Mellaril's side effects). This woman was a veritable cornucopia of anti-this, anti-that, and anti-the-other-thing medications, yet she was still depressed, anxious, agitated, and sick. Frankly, if any physician told me that I was to take all those medications, I'd run. Yet by common standards, Jane was getting the best medical care available.

Jane had a history of anorexia when she was in her teens, and she reported that she was once again experiencing a severe loss of appetite and that all she really wanted to do was drink. Despite the fact that she was eating less, she was now fifteen pounds overweight, with marked swelling of her hands and feet.

Physically, Jane felt awful. She had difficulty urinating, even though her bladder seemed to be full a great deal of the time. Constipation had become a chronic problem, so that she had to take laxatives in order to have a normal bowel movement. Although she found it nearly impossible to get out of bed in the morning, she was unable to fall asleep at night, and when she did sleep was restless with frequent periods of wakefulness. She was tired all the time and looked pale, pasty, and bloated.

Jane's mother had died of alcoholism, and a detailed drinking history revealed that Jane herself had been abusing alcohol for at least the past five years. Her physical exam revealed serious high blood pressure (despite the diuretics) as well as overweight. Her laboratory work showed that Jane was anemic, with seriously swollen and misshapen red blood cells. Her liver enzymes were elevated, and she was hypersecreting insulin.

Nutritionally, Jane was a mess. In addition to anemia and a very low vitamin B_{12} level, Jane's folic acid, vitamin E, zinc, thiamine, calcium, and potassium levels were well below normal. In general, she was severely malnourished with marked vitamin and mineral deficiencies that were only complicated and worsened by her severe allergies to corn, wheat, malt, yeast, beef, and eggs (all of which were major parts of her diet). She was also highly allergic to a variety of environmental agents— most notably molds. Jane was not in severe denial, fortunately, and was a very willing and active patient. The detoxification period was long and complex, since she had been on so many medications for so long. Even after she was detoxified from alcohol, it took us nearly two months to get her completely off Xanax, since all the benzodiazepines stay in the body for much longer than alcohol. Jane was placed on a diet which was free of sugar, refined carbohydrates, caffeine, and all the foods to which she was allergic. We helped her to establish a schedule of frequent small meals, and taught her how to maintain a healthful diet using fresh fruits, vegetables, and protein sources other than beef. Jane had no concept of how to read between the lines of product labels, so we taught her how to shop for foods without refined carbohydrates, preservatives, and her specific allergens—particularly corn syrup, which is used in an astonishing array of foods. To restore Jane's nutritional state, we placed her on intensive nutrient supplements (intramuscular to start), both multivitamins and specific supplementation of vitamin B_{12} and folic acid. Jane had become very withdrawn from her family and friends, so we encouraged her to be involved in family therapy, as well as group and individual counseling.

As Jane's brain cleared of the effects of alcohol and all the drugs she had been taking, she began to truly feel the impact of her father's death. Much of her time in individual counseling was spent working through this long overdue grief reaction.

When designing Jane's exercise program, the treatment team decided to capitalize on her interest in dance as a way to get her both physically and socially active. Jane had studied ballet and modern dance up until her teens, and had maintained an interest in both as an adult. Jane's renewed involvement in dance classes did much to improve both her physical condition and her outlook on life.

Despite all these breakthroughs, Jane remained strongly resistant to AA. She was an atheist and considered AA's concept of a Higher Power to be a form of organized religion. Despite our assurances that AA was not a religious organization and that Higher Power referred to different concepts for different people, Jane steadfastly refused to go to meetings.

Within three months Jane was free of all her psychological and physical symptoms, including the recurrent allergic reactions. Her weight was down, her energy level was up, and her relationships with family and friends had become active and vital once again. She was particularly happy to "not have to take all those bloody pills," and rather enjoyed the challenge of "nosing out" foods that contained corn, wheat, and the other foods to which she was allergic. Today, several years after she first came into my office a depressed, anxious, overmedicated wreck, Jane remains physically and psychologically stable. She has cut down on her work as an illustrator and now also works part time as an instructor at the gym where she began taking dance classes.

There are several elements of Jane's case that bear particular notice. If we had looked only at her psychological symptoms without investigating her drinking and family histories and doing a complete physical and biochemical evaluation, Jane would undoubtedly have been misdiagnosed yet again. If we had not detoxified her from *all* the drugs she was taking she would never have regained normal brain function. If we had not completely restored her—biochemically, nutritionally, and immunologically—she would have continued to feel depressed and unwell even without the drugs and alcohol. And if we had not continued this treatment for twelve months after her discharge from the hospital, it is doubtful that she would have been able to maintain the major life-style changes needed to live a life of serene sobriety. Even though Jane chose not to go to Alcoholics Anonymous, it was possible for her to get and stay sober. Alcoholic patients such as Jane need treatment that addresses all of their disease—body, mind, and spirit—regardless of whether or not they join AA.

15

OTHER DRUGS

Alcoholism is the most widespread and serious form of drug abuse in this country, but it is far from the only one. Illicit drugs have been a problem in many societies for most of history, but the problem has reached epidemic proportions over the last two decades.

There has been a lot of table-thumping rhetoric lately about the war on drugs. Calls to action ring in the halls of Congress, and various budgets are put forth for identifying, prosecuting, and punishing drug growers, producers, smugglers, dealers, and users. Interestingly, precious little is being allocated for actually treating drug abusers or preventing future drug use. Many of these noble goals are tangled in bureaucratic red tape and logistical problems ("Where," ask prison officials, "are we supposed to *put* all these people once you've arrested them?"), others are simply unrealistic. Few are being realized. The war on drugs seems to be a largely losing battle.

Why?

The generals of this war have forgotten a basic principle of economics: the crucial interplay of supply and demand. The drug industry, like the alcohol and tobacco industries, is a *business*. There is a tremendous demand for the various drugs that flood our streets, and this demand is just another manifestation of our society's obsession with the quick fix. Until this fundamental attitude is changed, drug dealers will find a rich market for their wares.

It is doubtful whether we will ever succeed in completely eradicating the market for illegal drugs, particularly since we have such a fondness for legal ones. But we can at least promote informed consumerism about drug use, be it legal or illegal. No intelligent person should take something into his or her body without knowing its effects and their duration. I have seen grown men refuse to try a new food until they were told what was in it, and then inhale an after-dinner line of white powder they'd bought from a complete stranger. We need to develop some healthy skepticism and discernment about drugs if we are ever to be really free of the yoke of drug addiction.

Not all drugs are created equal. Some—such as crack (a highly concentrated, smokable form of cocaine)—are almost instantly addictive. Others—such as alcohol—may take repeated use before an addiction develops. Some—such as many of the hallucinogens—are easily abused but rarely result in true addiction. The more you know about the various classes of drugs and their effects and risks, the more effective you can be in preventing dangerous drug use and experimentation by your children.

The following pages are by no means a complete explanation

of the various drugs of abuse. They will, however, provide you with an overview of the other drugs than can be involved in your loved one's problem.[1,2] In today's world, alcoholism rarely exists alone, particularly in young people. However, alcoholism is the underlying addiction in the majority of drug abuse cases, and alcohol is the primary gateway drug of our time.

THE DEPRESSANTS

The various depressant drugs (which include alcohol) exert their effects by slowing down the central nervous, respiratory, and cardiovascular systems. Medically, they are used in the treatment of a variety of conditions including anxiety, depres-

EXAMPLES OF DEPRESSANT DRUGS

Class	Chemical Name	Trade Name
barbiturate	secobarbitol	Seconal
	pentobarbital	Nembutal
piperidinedione	glutethimide	Doriden
	methyprylon	Noludar
tertiary alcohol	ethchlorvynol	Placidyl
quinazolinone	methaqualone	Quaalude (no longer commercially produced or sold)
benzodiazepine	lorazepam	Ativan
	clorazepate	Tranxene
	chlordiazepoxide	Librium
	oxazepam	Serax
	alprazolam	Xanax
	diazepam	Valium
carbamate	meprobamate	Miltown

sion, hypertension, epilepsy, insomnia, and muscular tension.

The popularity of the depressants is the result of their relaxing effects. In small doses, these drugs make the user feel calm, relaxed, and happy. At higher doses they can induce sleep, as well as a paradoxical reaction of violent rage.

Depressant overdose can result in a fatal suppression of breathing and heart rate. The risk of such an overdose is particularly acute when people combine depressant drugs such as Quaalude or Valium with alcohol.

The depressants are particularly dangerous because with increased use, higher and higher doses are needed to obtain the desired effect. Unfortunately, this tolerance to the subjective (intoxicating and calming) effects of the depressants is *not* accompanied by a physical tolerance. The toxic dose for the heavy user is almost the same as that for a first time user. As a result, persons addicted to the depressants are in ever-increasing danger of taking a toxic dose of the drug, particularly if they drink while on depressants. The fatal combination of depressant pills and alcohol has been implicated in a number of tragic deaths, including those of Judy Garland, Marilyn Monroe, and Abbie Hoffman.

The additive effect of the depressant drugs is one of the main reasons that I strongly discourage the use of Valium or any of the benzodiazepine tranquilizers in alcoholism treatment. The benzodiazepines are highly addictive in their own right, and are much more difficult to withdraw from than alcohol. Researchers have found that it is possible to become addicted to Valium after only six weeks of regular prescription use. When these drugs are taken in combination with alcohol they can be lethal.

THE STIMULANTS

The stimulant drugs make the user feel more alert and energetic by exerting effects almost exactly the opposite of the depressants. In the brain, these drugs affect the balance of norepinephrine, dopamine, and serotonin, and lower the amounts of electrical current needed to produce rewarding effects in the brain. As a result, stimulant drugs can make the user feel euphoric and powerful. Prolonged use can result in impotence and many other sexual dysfunctions and aberra-

EXAMPLES OF STIMULANT DRUGS

Drug	Trade Name	Street Name
amphetamine	Benzedrine	speed, bennies, black beauties
methamphetamine	Methadrine	crystal meth, crank, speed
dextroamphetamine	Dexadrine	dexies, Christmas trees
methylenedioxyamphet- amine	none	MDA, love drug
diet pills	Preludin, Tenuate, Fastin	black and whites
cocaine	none	coke, snow, blow, Bolivian marching powder, crack
caffeine	Folgers, Maxwell House (coffee); Lipton, Tetley (tea); Pepsi, Coca-Cola; OTC wakeup pills; Anacin, Extra-Strength Excedrin, some analgesics	java
nicotine	Winston, Marlboro, Salem (tobacco)	smoke, toke, stogies, cancer sticks

tions, but in the early stages of stimulant addiction sexual performance is often enhanced, leading to further use.

The stimulant drugs were once widely used as diet aids, but the rise in abuse of such diet pills has led to greater restraint in their use. Caffeine is frequently added to over-the-counter cold medications to counteract drowsiness, and stimulants are known to increase the potency of various analgesics and pain-killers. At present, the therapeutic medical uses of the stimulant drugs are relatively limited.

Tolerance to the rewarding effects of the stimulants (notably their euphoric actions) develops relatively quickly, leading the user to increase dosage in order to obtain the desired effect. In cocaine addiction, frequency of use increases, rather than the actual dosage.

Caffeine and nicotine are both extremely powerful stimulants, and their negative health effects are widely underestimated. Caffeinism, in particular, is frequently ignored by doctors and patients. Overuse of caffeine can result in drastic disruptions of normal sleep-wake cycles, a variety of gastrointestinal problems, and disruptions of blood sugar levels.

One of the most popular and deadly of the stimulant drugs is cocaine. Cocaine comes in a variety of forms and is derived from the leaves of the coca plant, which contain many drugs besides cocaine. Indians in Peru and Bolivia still use coca leaves (mixed with an alkali such as lime to activate the stimulant effect) as a medicine and stimulant. Coca leaves, unlike cocaine, contain many nutrients and must be chewed and digested, so that the actual amount of cocaine that is ingested is relatively small. The cocaine bought on the street is quite a different story.

When cocaine was identified and isolated from the coca leaf, it became popular very quickly. Physicians found it useful as a local anesthetic for surgery, particularly of the eyes and nose, and doctors prescribed cocaine for a variety of illnesses, including alcohol and opiate addiction. Sigmund Freud was an early advocate of cocaine's therapeutic uses.

It was not until the early 1900s that the abuse potential of cocaine began to be recognized, leading to a variety of laws restricting its use. Up until a few years ago it was still believed that cocaine was not physically addictive. We now know better. Cocaine passes the blood/brain barrier with ease, particularly when it is inhaled or smoked. In the brain, cocaine causes a range of neurochemical changes which result in a serious physical and psychological addiction. The highly concentrated forms of cocaine (such as crack and freebase) have such instant and dramatic effects on the brain that addiction is almost immediate.

Once in the brain, cocaine interferes with the reuptake of dopamine, serotonin, and norepinephrine. Put simply, cocaine causes more neurotransmitter to remain in the synapse so that the cells of the brain are hyperstimulated. The downside of this effect is directly proportional to its intensity: the higher you get, the farther you crash. Over time, the brain loses the ability to produce sufficient neurotransmitters to meet the cocaine-induced increase in demand. The cocaine user must take more cocaine at more frequent intervals to maintain even a semblance of normal brain function.

Over time, cocaine addiction results in a wide range of truly horrible psychological symptoms that can culminate in full-blown psychosis and violence. Cocaine also causes such severe cardiovascular arousal that even short-term use can be fatal. In prolonged addiction, permanent cardiac damage can result. Smoking cocaine causes a variety of bronchial complications, including bronchitis and pneumonia, and has also been known to cause a fatal paralysis of the respiratory system.

Cocaine, which was once thought of as a safe recreational drug, has proven to be one of the most dangerous drugs ever developed and a prime example of why we should not believe that any drug is risk free.

The Opiates

The opiate drugs, like cocaine, were originally derived from a plant, in this case the opium poppy. Of the twenty-plus drugs

THE OPIATES

Drug	Trade Name	Street Names
Opiates (natural derivatives)		
opium	none	"O"
codeine	various	number 3s (½ grain) number 4s (1 grain)
morphine	various	murphy, morph
heroin	none	smack, H, shit, junk, horse, scag
hydromorphone	Dilaudid	dillies
oxycodone	Percodan	percs
Opioids (synthetic)		
methadone	Dolophine	juice
propoxyphene	Darvon	pink ladies, pumpkin seeds
meperidine	Demerol	

that are found in this plant, two—morphine and codeine (methylmorphine)—have enjoyed widespread medical and recreational popularity in a variety of forms.

Morphine (named for Morpheus, the Greek god of sleep), was isolated in 1806 and was immediately hailed for its extraordinary power of pain relief. Morphine's calming effect protects the system from exhaustion in cases of traumatic shock, injury, or severe illness (such as typhoid fever). Various combinations and derivatives of the opium poppy have been developed for use as analgesics for most of recorded history, and all of them have tremendous abuse potential. The most notorious of these derivatives—heroin—produces the same effect as morphine in much smaller doses.

Heroin is the most well-known of the opiates, and heroin addicts (or junkies) have long been considered the prototype of drug addiction. Movies such as *Panic in Needle Park, The French Connection,* and *The Man with the Golden Arm* have encouraged the image of heroin as the greatest scourge of our society, and the deaths of famous heroin addicts such as Charlie "Bird" Parker, Billie Holliday, and Janis Joplin have seemed to confirm this view.

In actual fact, heroin is but one of the opiates that are currently being abused. Many more people are dependent on physician-prescribed opiates such as Percodan, Dilaudid, or Darvon than are addicted to street heroin. Heroin itself fell out of favor for a time, as cocaine came into the forefront. Nowadays, the mixture of heroin and cocaine—either simultaneously in the form of speedballs or in quick succession to enable the cocaine user to come down—is far more of a threat than heroin alone.

Tolerance, both physical and mental, develops quickly in the opiate abuser. Regular opiate users can tolerate doses of these drugs that would kill a first-time user. This characteristic of rapid tolerance sometimes leads regular opiate users to periodically kick the habit in order to lower their tolerance and increase the drug's effects.

It was research on the opiates that provided some of the most significant advances in our understanding of the neurochemistry of addiction. This research led to the discovery of the endorphins and enkephalins, the body's natural opiates. Opiate drugs literally fit into the receptor sites of these neurotransmitters and fool the brain into decreasing its natural production. When the drug is taken away, the brain and body cannot bounce back quickly enough, and withdrawal symptoms develop.

Physiologically, the opiate drugs generally depress the central nervous, respiratory, and digestive systems. Stomach and intestinal muscles relax, and digestive processes are slowed. The pupils contract, while breathing and heart rates diminish. Sexual function and hormonal secretions are also reduced.

In withdrawal, these systems hyperreact, so that users experience painful cramps, nausea, vomiting, and diarrhea, along with chills, sweating, rapid heart rate, runny nose, and severe muscle cramps throughout the body. Interestingly, opiate withdrawal, although it is highly unpleasant and dramatic, is usually not life threatening (except in infants.)

Complications from opiate addiction—particularly in intravenous users—are more of a threat, in some ways, than the actual drug. Chemical additives can increase a drug's potency, and wide variations in the actual concentration of opiate in any given street dose can lead to accidental overdose. Disease and vascular damage are a constant risk in intravenous users and skin poppers (who inject the drug under the skin rather than directly into a vein), and ulcers can develop in frequently used injection locations. Opiate addicts who snort heroin are subject to nasal perforations and damage, and opium smokers are at risk for a variety of bronchial ailments.

THE HALLUCINOGENS

The hallucinogens, particularly PCP and LSD, are equal (or at least a close second) to the opiates as the stereotypical bad drug. For many parents, finding out that their child is an acid head would be more devastating than hearing he or she had tried heroin. Word-of-mouth folk wisdom has promoted an image of all hallucinogens as chaos-producing chemicals that will make anyone who uses them believe he or she can fly and jump out the nearest window. The truth is a little more complicated.

Hallucinogens come in a variety of forms, both synthetic and natural, and have effects which range from dangerous delusions and hallucinations to mildly increased color acuity and sensitivity to touch. When synthetic hallucinogens such as LSD were first developed (and tested on college-student volunteers) there was a fairly plentiful supply of very potent, pure LSD on the market. Since LSD was legal, albeit experimental, in those early days, it enjoyed a great deal of popularity among young people. The altered states of consciousness that the drug produced were considered mind-expanding, and LSD continued to be popular well after it was made illegal. The potency and purity of these early batches of LSD and related drugs led to some of the more dramatic and tragic episodes associated with their use. Today, however, these drugs are no longer being produced by regular pharmaceutical companies, and true, potent, quality LSD is virtually impossible to find. Unfortunately, many of the drugs that have replaced it, most notably PCP, have even more dangerous effects.

The naturally occurring hallucinogens (such as various mushrooms and peyote) have been used in a variety of religious contexts in many societies throughout history. The altered states of consciousness and intense visual distortions and hallucinations produced by these substances were considered higher states of consciousness that brought the user close to whatever god or gods the society believed in. Contrast this with the more modern Western belief that these drugs induce temporary insanity. As such, hallucinogenic plants, or mixtures of such plants, were used in very circumscribed, controlled situations and not as recreational drugs.

The various hallucinogens, natural and synthetic, exert their effects on the central nervous and cardiovascular systems. Their popularity stems from their ability to produce states of awareness that are not normally experienced outside REM sleep. These experiences can range from unpleasant and dramatic hallucinations—such as those of giant bugs or melting walls—to a pleasant sensation of being one with the universe and being able to perceive people and things much more clearly. For example, being able to see into the atomic structure of the kitchen table, or watch the walls breathe. Some hallucinogens, such as MDA and various mushrooms, dramatically heighten sensitivity to touch, so that relatively mundane

THE HALLUCINOGENS

Chemical/Botanical Name	Drug	Street Name
Natural (botanical) Hallucinogens		
Lophophora williamsi	mescaline	mesc, big chief, cactus, peyote
Psilocybe cubensis	psilocybin	magic mushrooms, silly putty, 'shrooms
tetrahydrocannabinol	THC	pot, grass, weed, dope, reefer, ganja, hash oil, roach, hash
Banisteriopsis caapi	yage	
Myristica fragrans	nutmeg	
Atropa belladonna	belladonna	
Catha edulis	khat	
Ipomoea violacea	morning glory seeds	
Synthetic Hallucinogens		
lysergic acid diethylamide	LSD	acid, big D, sugar, trips, cubes, etc.
2, 5-dimethoxy-4-methylamphetamine	DOM, STP	serenity, peace pill, tranquility
methylenedioxy-amphetamine	MDA	love
phencyclidine	PCP	angel dust
methylenedioxymethyl-amphetamine	MDMA	adam, XTC
dimethyltryptamine	DMT	businessman's trip

physical activities such as brushing one's hair or teeth become inordinately pleasurable.

Hallucinogenic "trips," as these experiences are called, last from between four and twelve hours. However, most of the hallucinogens are lipid soluble, and can be stored in the body's fat deposits for extended periods of time. In persons who have experienced a toxic reaction to hallucinogens (the bum trip described in numerous antidrug campaigns), flashbacks have been known to occur months after the last ingestion of the drug, perhaps as stored hallucinogen is released from fat deposits.

Physically, all the hallucinogens are strong stimulants, and some are so toxic that when taken orally they induce nausea and vomiting (peyote, for example). Activation of the sympathetic nervous system results in widely dilated pupils; decreased blood flow to the extremities; leading to a sensation of cold in these areas; as well as dizziness and weakness. Pulse rate and blood pressure are elevated, while body temperature drops. Common visual phenomenon are wavelike trails—not unlike those seen in photos of moving lights at night—following moving objects.

Physical tolerance to the hallucinogens develops quickly, so that the intensity of the experience is drastically reduced. Since the sensations induced by the hallucinogens are so dramatic and are generally fairly incapacitating, even die-hard fans tend to reserve their use for special occasions. Exceptions to this rule are so-called party drugs such as MDA and MDMA, which have less hallucinatory effects than LSD, mescaline, and the various botanicals. Two other notable exceptions are PCP and the cannabinols (marijuana, hashish, etc.)—which deserve separate discussion.

PCP. Phencyclidine was developed in the fifties for use as a surgical anesthetic, but was abandoned for use in humans when patients reported unpleasant mental and perceptual side effects. At present the drug is used as an anesthetic for animals.

PCP, because it is both easy and inexpensive to produce, is often mixed with or passed off as other drugs. Most "magic mushrooms" being sold in urban areas are actually Chinese mushrooms which have been coated or dusted with PCP.

PCP is well absorbed no matter how it is taken (very little is excreted in urine), and its effects vary depending on the dose. In small doses, PCP produces a feeling of disassociation from the body and reality. As dosage increases, this disassociation can be accompanied by apathy, disorganized thought, distorted perception of time and space, hostility, and eventually psychosis and violence. Since PCP users are essentially unaware of physical pain, they are exceptionally difficult to control or restrain when violent.

Physically, PCP causes increased heart rate, blood pressure, and body temperature, as well as profuse sweating and salivation. Limbs can become numb and rigid, and in higher doses seizures and convulsions can ensue.

While PCP is marketed as a drug in its own right, it is used as an additive to other drugs so frequently that many PCP users may not even be aware that they have taken it. When added to marijuana, or sold as mescaline or some other hallucinogen, PCP can cause quite different sensations that either of these drugs. Most psychedelic drugs that are currently available on the street contain at least some of this dangerous chemical.

Marijuana. The active component of marijuana is tetrahy-drocannabinol (THC)—a unique chemical that has some of the features of hallucinogens, stimulants, and depressants. THC's unique structure makes its effects highly variable. Some marijuana users find it makes them sleepy, others find it perks them up, while still others report that it produces mild psychedelic experiences. First-time users often feel nothing at all.

THC is lipid soluble, and its effects are felt most quickly if it is smoked. It can also be mixed with food. When taken orally, however, the rate of absorption can be uneven, and the risk of overdose is somewhat greater. Physically, THC results in increased heart rate, dry mouth and eyes, dilation of blood vessels (hence the reddened eyes typical of marijuana smokers), and a general loss of coordination and balance. Reaction time is also impaired.

Over time, marijuana use causes a variety of negative effects, including bronchial inflammation and changes in immune function, and can result in long-term changes in sleep and eating patterns.

THC's lipid solubility makes it particularly dangerous to fetal development. Prolonged marijuana use has been associated with negative changes in sperm motility, cellular metabolism, and cardiovascular function. Marijuana, while not quite the scourge of society that was portrayed in *Reefer Madness,* is far from a safe drug, particularly in young people who are still developing physically.

While the psychological effects of marijuana vary greatly, it commonly produces disinhibition, talkativeness, relaxation, euphoria, and drowsiness. Prolonged, habitual marijuana use has been linked to an amotivational syndrome characterized by low productivity, apathy, low frustration tolerance, and a general lack of interest in caring for oneself or one's interests. It is this amotivational syndrome that is characteristic of the pot head, as immortalized by comedians such as Cheech and Chong— the rather vague, sloppy, unbelievably mellow young person with no particular interest in anything but having another joint. This character, while amusing on screen, is tragic in a classroom or job situation.

When dealing with any illicit drug, it is important to remember that there is no way of knowing what you are actually buying. You cannot verify a drug dealer's honesty by calling the Better Business Bureau. It's fairly certain that any chemical bought on the street was produced in a filthy, ill-equipped, and highly illegal lab and mixed with lots of possibly dangerous additives. The penalties for possession of illegal drugs are becoming more severe, and risking several years in prison for a couple of milligrams of talcum powder and PCP is just plain stupid.

Legal drugs, such as alcohol and physician-prescribed tranquilizers and painkillers, carry their own risks. As a general rule, no one should take a drink or a pill until they fully understand the possible risks and benefits. Will the pill that helps you go to sleep make it hard for you get up? Will it keep you from dreaming? Are you only supposed to take it once a week? Will the tranquilizer that "smooths out the rough spots" also damage your liver if you take it for more than a month? Will the fourth scotch on the rocks finally pull your genetic-metabolic trigger for alcoholism? The human brain is a complex and wondrous organ, and there is no real way of knowing what a particular drug will do to its fragile balance. Drug use of any kind is a game of Russian roulette. If we learn to think before drinking or taking a pill, we are far less likely to fall into the trap of drug or alcohol addiction.

16

NUTRITIONAL PROGRAM

All alcoholics are malnourished to some degree. Even if they consume a relatively balanced diet, alcohol itself is an antinutrient which causes nutrients to be malabsorbed, poorly utilized, and excreted in greater amounts. Every alcoholic needs nutritional restoration, and every alcoholic should learn to live by the principles of good nutrition.

Recovering alcoholics have one nutritional advantage over the rest of us—they *know* they are malnourished. Most Americans exist in blissful ignorance of their own nutritional peril, eating junk food at irregular intervals and making no connection between their various ills and their dismal diets. But the fact remains that most of us do not eat well, and vast numbers of us are as malnourished as the alcoholic. The nutritional principles outlined in this chapter are applicable to everyone and should be applied to every member of the family, not just the alcoholic. Good nutrition is the cornerstone of a healthy life-style.

In some ways the body is like a car with an extremely delicate and powerful engine but a rather small gas tank. It needs fuel at very regular intervals if it is to run properly, and the fuel needs to be high octane and free of additives and contaminants. When we don't provide a constant, quality fuel supply, we develop the biological equivalent of engine knocks.

A quality food supply is one which provides for the nutritional needs of the body without altering the body's metabolic homeostasis. Refined carbohydrates and sugars, for example, upset the blood glucose balance. Excess fats that cannot be effectively removed by the body's normal lipid metabolism build up in arteries. Chemical additives and preservatives can trigger a number of toxic and allergic reactions.

The bodies which we inhabit in the twentieth century are not much different from the bodies our ancestors inhabited when they were roaming the plains as hunter-gatherers. Many of the foods which were rare treats at that time (most notably sweets, red meat, and eggs) are now daily parts of our diet. Our ancestors were forced to eat a variety of foods since their diet was determined by whatever was available and in season. In today's world of fast-frozen foods and easy transport, it is possible to eat the same foods every day, regardless of the season. Our ancestors had to chase down and kill their pot roasts. We simply walk to the supermarket. Our bodies are literally not designed to handle many of the foods we are eating so frequently and in such vast amounts. They need more variety, in more moderation. None of us are going to move out onto the veldt and start hunting gazelles and digging roots for dinner. But we can be more reasonable in the foods we choose to eat and the pattern in which we eat them. For the alcoholic, this nutritional program means proper nourishment and comfortable sobriety. For the nonalcoholic, it means a lifetime of good health. This basic nutritional program, a duplicate of that given to patients being discharged from Brunswick House, consists of five major components:

1. natural foods
2. a balanced diet
3. frequent small meals
4. elimination or reduction of: caffeine, sugar, refined carbohydrates, preservatives, additives, and foods which cause adverse symptoms
5. high quality vitamin/mineral supplements

BALANCED DIET
(INCLUDING A WIDE VARIETY OF FOODS)

It is impossible to fill all your body's nutritional needs if you eat only a few foods. Each day your diet should include foods from the following food groups:

- proteins (meat, fish, poultry, eggs)
- vegetables
- fruits
- bread, cereals, grains
- dairy foods (milk, yogurt, cheese)
- fats (oils, butter, nuts, and seeds)

Of these groups, protein is the best for maintaining blood sugar levels, and protein foods make much better between-meal snacks than candy bars or other sugary foods. Foods that are high in protein include meat, poultry, eggs, dairy foods, nuts, and seeds.

Not all protein foods are created equal, however. You have undoubtedly heard all the controversy over cholesterol and saturated fats, and some discretion should be used in choosing your protein sources. Red meats have more cholesterol than poultry (and contrary to certain advertising campaigns, pork is *not* a white meat) and should not be eaten every day. Dairy products vary widely in their fat content, so read labels. Cottage cheese (particularly when made with skim milk) is a good protein source with little fat. Nuts and seeds contain many essential fatty acids and are a terrific quick source of protein— but not if they have been deep fried and coated with a thick layer of salt. Whenever possible, eat foods that are as close to their natural state as possible.

Variety is crucial to good nutrition. Even if you love broccoli, don't eat it at every meal. Give yourself variety in all your food choices. Stock several types of vegetables, fruits, cereals, meats, etc. in your larder and try to limit your consumption of any particular food to once every three days or so. (Please note, eating macaroni on Tuesday, spaghetti on Wednesday, and lasagna on Thursday does not count as maintaining variety— pasta is pasta, no matter what shape it's in.)

SMALL FREQUENT MEALS

The longer the body goes without food, the more likely the blood sugar levels are to fall. Eating a small snack between meals will help maintain the blood sugar at adequate levels. Try to eat something every two to three hours. Good snacks include cheese, nuts or seeds, small pieces of meat or poultry, and fruit.

ELIMINATE OR REDUCE CONSUMPTION OF SUGAR AND SUGAR-CONTAINING FOODS AND CAFFEINE

Sugar is found in far more places than the sugar bowl. The average American consumes 130 pounds of sugar a year. Most of this comes from processed foods to which sugar has been added. The only way to know what is in the food you are eating is to *read labels*! Words that mean sugar include:

- sucrose
- dextrose
- lactose
- sorbitol
- mannitol
- dextrins
- corn syrup
- maple syrup
- brown sugar
- raw sugar
- invert sugar
- turbinado sugar
- honey

Natural sugars such as honey and maple syrup have similar effects on the body as table sugar (sucrose) so they, too, should be avoided. If you wish to add a sweetener to food, use fruit juice, Sweet'N Low or Equal (Note: Equal contains corn and should be avoided by those who have an allergy to corn). Some foods such as bread almost always have some sweetener added. Try to select ones where the sugar is found at the end or near the end of the ingredient list (ingredients are listed in descending order of their quantities, the highest first).

Because of caffeine's effect on the blood sugar, limit the daily intake to one to two cups of regular coffee or tea. You may drink as much decaffeinated coffee or tea as you want. Caffeine is also found in cola drinks, Ovaltine, chocolate, and the following medications: Anacin, A.P.C., A.S.A. Compound, Cafergot, Coricidin, Empirin Compound, Fiorinal, Pamprin, Trigesic.

Use plain aspirin, Bufferin, or Tylenol.

ELIMINATE OR REDUCE THE INTAKE OF HIGHLY PROCESSED FOODS INCLUDING REFINED CARBOHYDRATES

Processed foods have been altered in some way from their original state and generally contain far less vitamins and minerals and far more additives and artificial ingredients than unprocessed foods. Highly processed foods include TV dinners, most packaged snack foods, canned goods, nondairy creamers, refined carbohydrates, etc. (see list of foods allowed and foods to avoid, p. 235). Refined carbohydrates include white bread, white rice, and white pasta. Choose whole grain breads and cereals, brown rice, whole wheat pasta or semolina flour pasta (available in most health food stores and some supermarkets). When reading labels, choose those that say whole wheat flour, soy flour, oat flour, rye flour, corn flour, semolina, etc. Avoid those that say white flour, enriched white flour, unbleached flour, enriched unbleached flour, wheat flour, or enriched wheat flour. Whole grains do not need to be enriched. If it says "enriched," do not buy it.

ELIMINATE OR ROTATE
ANY KNOWN ALLERGY-PRODUCING FOODS

If the individual has been tested or is aware of any food hypersensitivities, these foods should either be removed from the diet or rotated (eaten no more than once every four days).

TAKE A HIGH QUALITY
VITAMIN/MINERAL SUPPLEMENT

Recovering alcoholics have depleted their nutritional stores. Vitamin/mineral supplementation helps meet these increased nutritional needs and should be continued for at least the first year of sobriety. Some possible supplements include:

- Roche Laboratories' Berocca Plus Nutrient Supplement; dosage: one capsule three times a day
- Twin Laboratories' Allergy Multi Caps; dosage: two capsules three times a day
- Bronson's Fortified Insurance Formula; dosage: two capsules three times a day
- calcium with magnesium to equal 1,000 milligrams calcium, 500 milligrams magnesium daily [calcium citrate by Twin Labs is recommended]
- time-release niacin supplements

- *amino acid preparations* (helps restore neurotransmitter balance) such as Matrix Technologies' Saave; dosage: two tablets twice a day between meals
- l-glutamine (an amino acid that reduces alcohol craving); dosage: 1000 milligrams three times a day between meals

Use the following as a guide in making food selections:

Foods	To Include	To Avoid
meat, fish, fowl	fresh or frozen; canned fish packed in water allowed, although fresh fish is better; tuna, mackerel, or swordfish at least once a week	salted, processed, smoked, or breaded meats, croquettes, meat pies (using refined flour), sausages, frankfurters, cold cuts
milk	whole, skim, buttermilk, powdered milk, half and half	condensed milk, nondairy creamer
potato or substitutes	fresh potatoes, whole kernel corn, wild or brown rice, whole grain pasta	white rice, white pasta, instant potatoes, potato chips, Cracker Jacks
soup	homemade soups with allowed ingredients: consomme, meat, and vegetables	creamed soups, all commercial soups, canned and frozen, soup base, bouillon cubes
sweets	Sweet 'N Low; Nutrasweet, aspartame; make homemade desserts and sweeten with fruit juice	sugar and sweets

Foods	To Include	To Avoid
vegetables	fresh or frozen; fresh vegetables juices	canned vegetables, sauerkraut and other vegetables preserved in salt brine, canned vegetable juices
miscellaneous	spices, herbs, and seeds as tolerated; nuts, brewer's yeast; peanut butter with no sugar or additives	catsup, barbecue sauce, tartar sauce, tortilla chips, corn chips, cheese doodles, pickles, relishes, meat extracts, commercially prepared sauces; all flavoring extracts
beverages	decaffeinated coffee or tea, herbal teas, water, seltzer, club soda	excessive consumption of caffeinated coffee or tea (limit to one to two cups daily), drink mixers, cocoa, colas, regular sodas, malt, ovaltine, fruit juices and fruit drink with added sugar, Postum
breads, grains, and cereals	whole grains and flours, such as millet, oats, barley, whole wheat, rice, corn, wheat germ, soy, rye, buckwheat; homemade pancakes or waffles with allowed ingredients (shredded wheat, Kellogg's Nutri-Grain, puffed wheat)	refined white bread, enriched flours, commercial mixes, frozen waffles and pancakes; muffins, doughnuts, pastries, sweetrolls, rusk, zweiback, matzoh, crackers (unless from whole grains)
cheese	plain cottage cheese, swiss, cream cheese, Monterey Jack, caraway, Cheddar, farmer, ricotta, Muenster, and other hard, unprocessed cheese	smoked cheese, cheese foods, cheese dips and spreads, American, Velveeta, and any processed cheese

Foods	To Include	To Avoid
eggs	fresh eggs	Eggbeaters
fats	butter and vegetable oils, Paul Newman's Own and Marie's Blue Cheese salad dressings, Balance mayonnaise	margarine, gravies, commercial salad dressings
fruits and fruit juices	fresh, canned, or frozen without sugar; unsulfured dried fruits; 100 percent fruit juices; fresh, canned, or frozen (limit juice to 8 ounces a day)	fruit and fruit juices canned or frozen, sugar or preservatives, dried fruits with sulfured preservatives

To season foods you may use lemon, lime, salt, pepper, any spices such as garlic, onion powder, ginger, nutmeg, parsley, etc., that do not contain sugars or artificial additives. If you wish to use soy sauce buy tamari in a health food store, which is naturally processed.

Sample Menu

Below is a sample of a day's menu, which includes three average meals with high protein snacks in between. This is only an example and does not take into account individual preferences or food allergies.

Breakfast (7 A.M.)
juice or fruit
eggs or whole grain cereal
whole grain toast with butter
milk (whole, low fat, or skim)
coffee or tea

Mid-morning Snack (10 A.M.)
cheese and fruit or nuts and fruit

Lunch (noon)
meat, fish, or poultry
salad with oil and vinegar or allowed dressing
cooked vegetable
whole grain bread with butter
fresh fruit
milk
decaffeinated coffee or tea

Mid-afternoon Snack (3 P.M.)
cheese and raw vegetables or nuts and fruit
seltzer with lime

Dinner (6 P.M.)
homemade soup prepared with allowed ingredients
meat, fish, or poultry
salad with allowed dressing
cooked vegetable
baked potato or brown rice

fresh fruit
decaffeinated coffee or tea

Evening Snack (8 P.M.)
plain yogurt with fresh fruit
milkshake made with fresh fruit, ice cubes, fruit juice
cheese or nuts

17
WHERE TO GET HELP

Every community has its own assortment of support groups, hot lines, help lines, and referral sources. Numbers for these groups are usually available in the local telephone directory. Numbers for local hot lines and crisis intervention are particularly important, since national toll-free hot lines are few and far between.

Of the many private and public programs for alcoholics and their families, the two most widespread and successful are Alcoholics Anonymous and Al-Anon (which includes Alateen). Local numbers for these groups can be found in the yellow and white pages.

Alcoholics Anonymous
P.O. Box 459
Grand Central Station
New York, NY 10163
(212)473-6200 (9 A.M. to 10 P.M. EST Monday through

Saturday; noon to 10 P.M. Sunday; answering machine on all other times)

AA is a fellowship of individuals who share their experiences, strength, and hope to solve their common problem of alcoholism and to help others with the disease. The only requirement for membership is the desire to stop drinking. There are no dues or fees. AA is not affiliated with any sect, faith, or political group, and all members are geared entirely toward the goal of staying sober and helping others achieve sobriety.

AA pioneered the concept of alcoholism as a disease of the body, mind, and spirit, and hypothesized early on that alcoholism might be a manifestation of some form of allergy to alcohol. Current research is proving at least some connection between allergy and alcoholism. Many of AA's principles and axioms (such as HALT) show an astonishing understanding of the biological complexity of alcoholism.

Over the years, AA has grown somewhat away from the early recognition of the importance of biology and nutrition in alcoholism, but it should still be a crucial part of any alcoholic's recovery process. Some basic precautions should be taken to make AA work best for you, however. For example, it would be wise to either avoid groups that serve sugary snacks and caffeinated coffee at their meetings or to bring healthy snacks and beverages of your own instead. Some AA members may advise you to have a candy bar when you crave alcohol. Remember that sugar is as bad for your glucose metabolism as alcohol; have a protein snack instead.

There are many AA groups which now serve decaffeinated coffee and sugar-free snacks at their meetings, and smoke-free meetings are also available. This increased interest in health and nutrition is a very positive move that actually fulfills the vision of AA's founder, Bill W.

During my study of AA's history I was fortunate enough to get to know Dr. Abram Hoffer of Vancouver, Canada. Dr. Hoffer had been Bill W.'s personal physician, and he told me that shortly before Bill's death from emphysema he had said that AA's one drawback was that it had not paid attention to the dangers of sugar, caffeine, and cigarettes. It is encouraging that so many AA members are now recognizing these dangers.

Some people may have difficulty accepting the concept of a Higher Power that is one of the cornerstones of AA's steps and traditions. For many AA members, this Higher Power is basically the Judeo-Christian concept of God. There are, however, many Buddhist, Muslim, and even atheist members of Alcoholics Anonymous, and the Higher Power can have many definitions. The important thing is to realize that alcoholism cannot be defeated simply by the exercise of will and that if you rely entirely on your own resources to defeat it you will probably fail. The Higher Power that you draw on for strength and support can be God, the universe, the collected caring of the people you love, a dead relative, even the oak tree in your backyard.

The anonymity of AA members is key to the identity of AA, and should be respected and adhered to. Anonymity allows each member to feel safe and secure—free to tell his or her story without fear of being betrayed. Recovery depends on being able to tell your own story, honestly, in the supportive presence of others; and to receive loving, honest feedback and help. Anonymity promotes humility as well as honesty and ensures that members are coming together on the common ground of alcoholism, regardless of their position in society. In Alcoholics Anonymous, Liz T. of Topeka, Kansas, is no different from Liz T. of Hollywood, California.

Al-Anon/Alateen

P.O. Box 862
Midtown Station
New York, NY 10018-0862
(212)302-7240 (9 A.M. to 5 P.M. EST)
1-800-356-9996 (24 hours)

Al-Anon and Alateen are fellowships of men, women, and children whose lives have been affected by the compulsive drinking of a family member or friend. Their purpose is to help these individuals, regardless of whether or not the alcoholic has found sobriety.

Al-Anon and Alateen make use of the same steps and traditions as AA to provide comfort, hope, and friendship to its members. Members share their experiences and situations to find new and healthy ways to deal with their loved ones' alcoholism by focusing on themselves instead of the alcoholics. Members learn that their growth and serenity depends on not criticizing the alcoholic or focusing on his or her shortcomings. Al-Anon members assist each other in developing intervention strategies and in learning to detach themselves from the web of alcoholism that envelops the alcoholic.

If you cannot find a listing for Al-Anon in your area, the national office can refer you to local groups.

National Association of Children of Alcoholics

31582 Coast Highway (Suite B)

South Laguna, CA 92677

(714)499-3889 (9 A.M. to 5 P.M. PST)

NACOA is a loose affiliation of groups devoted to assisting the children of alcoholic families, regardless of their age or drinking habits, to cope with the emotional and psychological issues of growing up with an alcoholic parent. The national office can refer you to therapists in your area that specialize in these issues, as well as local contacts for free NACOA meetings.

National Institute of Drug Abuse Hot Line

1-800-662-HELP(4537) (9 A.M. to 3 A.M. EST)

This help line is the only toll-free hot line available nationally that provides counseling and phone crisis intervention in addition to information services. The staff members are extremely helpful and understanding—a good referral source, as well. The phone lines are manned eighteen hours a day, although during business hours you may be put on hold for a very short time. Staff members are also able to give you the names and numbers of treatment hospitals in your area that match your financial situation.

The following organizations can provide information about alcoholism and alcoholism information programs.

National Clearinghouse for Drug & Alcohol Abuse Information

P.O. Box 2345

Rockville, MD 20852

(301)468-2600 (8:30 A.M. to 5 P.M. EST)

Distributes publications by the National Institute on Drug Abuse. Can do literature searches on alcoholism and other drug issues. Can also provide referrals to other agencies and state clearing houses on these topics.

National Council on Alcoholism
12 W. 21 Street (8th floor)
New York, NY 10010
1-800-NCA-CALL (1-800-621-2155) (9 A.M. to 5 P.M. EST)

Information and referral service on alcoholism and alcohol-related topics. Some information on treatment and support groups.

Mothers Against Drunk Driving (MADD)
669 Airport Freeway
Suite 310
Hurst, TX 76053
(817)268-6233 (9 A.M. to 5 P.M.)
1-800-438-6233 (Victim hot line 24 hours)

National organization geared to the prevention of drunk driving. Has educational programs for elementary through high school students, as well as national programs promoting safe driving habits.

Students Against Driving Drunk (SADD)
P.O. Box 800
Marlboro, MA 01752
(508)481-3568 (9 A.M. to 5 P.M. EST)

National organization of students dedicated to the prevention of drunk driving. Has elementary programs and curricula designed for high school through college ages. Has resulted in the development of programs such as "designated drivers," and taxi services for those who feel they are too drunk to drive.

NOTES

2. Alcoholism—An Overview

1. The statistics on alcoholism and alcohol-related problems were taken from a fact sheet compiled by the National Council on Alcoholism, Inc. (NCA), the national nonprofit organization combating alcoholism, other drug addictions, and related problems. "Founded in 1944, NCA's major programs include prevention and education, public information, medical-scientific information, public policy advocacy, conferences and publications. NCA's network of about two hundred state and local nonprofit affiliates conduct similar activities in their areas and provide information and referral services to families and individuals seeking help with alcohol or other drug problems. . . . The organization sponsors a national toll-free telephone number 1-800-NCA-CALL. Callers are mailed the address and telephone number of the nearest NCA affiliate or other referral resource and basic information about alcoholism."

2. The 1964 study was a joint effort of the American Hospital Association and the National Institute of Mental Health. Of the 5200 hospitals which returned questionnaires, more than 3200 refused admission to patients with acute or chronic alcoholism.

3. The House of Delegates adopted the statement on alcoholism at its 1956 Clinical Convention. In the statement, the delegates asserted that "alcoholic symptomatology . . . comes within the scope of medical practice [and] . . . places the alcoholic in the category of a sick individual." Further, the delegates noted that "the individual patient should be evaluated rather than have general objection on the grounds of a diagnosis of alcoholism."

4. The proposed alcoholism curriculum was sent out to medical schools on April 8, 1959.

5. The AMA House of Delegates voted to reaffirm the 1956 statement on the admission of alcoholics to general hospitals at its 1966 Clinical Meeting. The decision to reaffirm the statement may have been the result of earlier findings by the Committee on Medical Facilities. This committee reviewed all the publications and bulletins of the Joint Commission On Accreditation of Hospitals in the years since 1956. They found that the commission had done nothing to officially encourage hospitals to "take a more active interest in meeting the alcoholism problem."

6. *The Diagnostic and Statistical Manual* is the official manual of the American Psychiatric Association. It details the specific diagnoses and syndromes of psychiatric disorders, and is periodically revised and updated to keep up with current research information. The definition used in the text is from the third edition—revised.

7. Williams, R. H. "Treatment of Alcoholism." *Consumers' Research* (December 1985), pp. 16–19. The breakdown of the fate of one hundred alcoholics was based on data for the Washington, D.C., metropolitan area.

8. Mendelson, J.H., et al. "Hospital Treatment of Alcoholism: A Profile of Middle-Income Americans." *Alcoholism: Clinical and Experimental Research*, Vol. 6, No. 3 (1980), pp. 377–383.

9. Gordis, E., et al. "Outcome of Alcoholism Treatment among 5578 Patients in an Urban Comprehensive Hospital-Based Program:

Application of a Computerized Data System." *Alcoholism: Clinical and Experimental Research*, Vol. 5, No. 4 (1981), pp. 509–522.

10. Emrick, C.D. "A Review of Psychologically Oriented Treatment Programs of Alcoholism II: The Relative Effectiveness of Different Treatment Approaches and the Effectiveness of Treatment versus No Treatment." *Journal of Studies on Alcohol*, Vol. 36, No. 1 (1975), pp. 88–108.

11. Helzer, J. E., et al. "The Extent of Long-Term Moderate Drinking among Alcoholics Discharged from Medical and Psychiatric Treatment Facilities." *New England Journal of Medicine*, Vol. 312, No. 26 (1985), pp. 1678–1682.

12. Guenther, R. M. "The Role of Nutritional Therapy in Alcoholism Treatment." *International Journal of Biosocial Research*, Vol. 4, No. 1(1983), pp. 5–18.

13. Beasley, J. D., et al. "Evaluation of Efficacy of a Comprehensive Bio-Behavioral Model for the Treatment of Patients with Severe Alcohol Dependence Syndrome." Submitted for publication, 1989.

3. Alternative "Highs"—The Natural Way

1. Ross, D. L. "Ad Spending Cutbacks Hit All Alcoholic Beverages." *Impact*, Vol. 18, Nos. 15 and 16 (1988), pp. 1–11. Additional thanks to the Center for Science in the Public Interest for their assistance in locating this information.

2. Despite advertising to the contrary, a large percentage of Americans are nutritionally compromised. In 1982, the Institute of Medicine estimated that one out of every six American men was frankly obese (20 percent or more overweight). In women the figure rose to 25 percent. Despite the added weight, many of these people are severely malnourished. The government's Health and Nutrition Examination Survey II (carried out between 1976 and 1980) found that:

- 25 percent of all women (ages fifteen to seventy-four) don't get enough protein
- 75 percent of twelve- to eighteen-year-old girls have deficient calcium intake; the same is true of 25 percent of all males
- 25 percent of all Americans are deficient in vitamin C
- 95 percent of all women over thirty-five have deficient iron intake.

3. In 1973, Roger Williams investigated the nutritional value of enriched wheat bread. He fed a group of lab rats nothing but enriched white bread for ninety days. At the end of that period, two thirds of the animals were dead of malnutrition. The others were severely stunted.

4. Ross, D. L. "Koop's Panel Stirs Controversy Over Alcohol Ads." *Impact*, Vol. 19, No. 3 (1989), pp. 1–4.

4. Genetics

1. See Beasley, chapter 2, reference 13.

2. Goodwin, D. W. "Is Alcoholism Hereditary?" *Archives of General Psychiatry*, Vol. 25 (1971), pp. 545–549.
Cadoret, R. J. "Development of Alcoholism in Adoptees Raised Apart from Alcoholic Biological Relatives." *Archives of General Psychiatry*, Vol. 37 (1980), pp. 561–563.

3. Kaij, L. "Studies on the Etiology and Sequels of Abuse of Alcohol." Department of Psychiatry, University of Lund, Sweden, 1960.
Hrubec, Z., and Omenn, G. S. "Evidence of Genetic Predisposition to Alcoholic Cirrhosis and Psychosis: Twin Concordances for Alcoholism and Its Biological End Points by Zygosity among Male Veterans." *Alcoholism: Clinical and Experimental Research*, Vol. 5, No. 2 (1981), pp. 207–215.

4. See Goodwin, above.

5. Wolff, P. H. "Ethnic Differences in Alcohol Sensitivity." *Science,* Vol. 175 (1972), pp. 440–450.

Harada, S., Agarwal, D. P., et al. "Aldehyde Dehydrogenase Isozyme Variation and Alcoholism in Japan." *Pharmacology, Biochemistry and Behavior,* Vol. 18, Suppl. 1 (1983), pp. 151–153.

Suwaki, H. and Ohara, H. "Alcohol-Induced Facial Flushing and Drinking Behavior in Japanese Men." *Journal of Studies on Alcohol,* Vol. 46, No. 3 (1985), pp. 196–198.

6. Schuckit, M. A., and Gold, M. "A Simultaneous Evaluation of Multiple Markers of Ethanol/Placebo Challenges in Sons of Alcoholics and Controls." *Archives of General Psychiatry,* Vol. 45 (1988), pp. 211–216.

7. Begleiter, H., et al. "Event-Related Brain Potentials in Boys at Risk for Alcoholism." *Science,* Vol. 225, No. 4669 (1984), pp. 1493–1496.

Gabrielli, W. F., et al. "Electroencephalograms in Children of Alcoholic Fathers." *Psychophysiology,* Vol. 19, No. 4 (1982), pp. 404–407.

Pollock, V. E., et al. "The EEG after Alcohol Administration in Men at High Risk for Alcoholism." *Archives of General Psychiatry,* Vol. 58, No. 4 (1983), pp. 316–321.

8. Schuckit, M. A., and Rayses, V. "Ethanol Ingestion: Differences in Blood Acetaldehyde Concentrations in Relatives of Alcoholics and Controls." *Science,* Vol. 203 (1979), pp. 54–55.

5. Tolerance and Addiction

1. Lieber, C. S. "The Metabolism of Alcohol." *Scientific American,* Vol. 234, No. 3 (1976), pp. 25–33. The seminal work on the

effect of alcohol on the liver and the development of the microsomal ethanol oxidizing system.

2. Blum, K., et al. "Putative Role of Isoquinoline Alkaloids in Alcoholism. A Link to Opiates." *Alcoholism*, Vol. 2 (1978), pp. 113–120.

Collins, M.A., et al. "Dopamine-Related Tetrahydroisoquinolines: Significant Urinary Excretion by Alcoholics after Alcohol Consumption." *Science*, Vol. 206 (1979), pp. 1184–1186.

3. Genazzini, A. R., et al. "Central Deficiency of Beta-Endorphin in Alcohol Addicts." *Journal of Clinical Endocrine Metabolism*, Vol. 55, No. 3 (September 1982), pp. 583–586.

Govoni, S., et al. "Heavy Drinking Decreases Plasma Metenkephalin Concentrations." *Alcohol and Drug Research*, Vol. 7, No. 2 (1987), pp. 93–98.

4. Kent, T. A., et al. "Blood Platelet Uptake of Serotonin in Men Alcoholics." *Journal of Studies on Alcohol*, Vol. 46, No. 4 (1985), pp. 357–359.

Ballenger, J., et al. "Alcohol and Central Serotonin Metabolism in Man." *Archives of General Psychiatry*, Vol. 36 (1979), pp. 224–227.

6. Malnutrition and Toxicity

1. Kissin, B., and Begleiter, H., eds. *The Biology of Alcoholism*. New York: Plenum Press, 1972 and following. This multivolume set covers every aspect of the disease of alcoholism. Volume I: *Biochemistry* contains a complete and impressive collection of data on alcohol's effects from the disruption of cell membranes to the exact chemistry of various alcoholic beverages. The series is, however, geared very much to the scientist or physician.

Sherlock, S. "Nutrition and the Alcoholic." *Lancet*, Vol. 8374 (February 25, 1984), pp. 436–439.

2. Dornhost, A., and Ouyang, A. "The Effect of Alcohol on Glucose Tolerance." *Lancet* (October 30, 1971), pp. 957–959.

Marks, V. "Alcohol and Changes in Body Constituents: Glucose and Hormones." *Proceedings of the Royal Society of Medicine,* Vol. 68, No. 6 (1975), pp. 377–380.

Metz, R., et al. "Potentiation of the Plasma Insulin Response to Glucose by Prior Administration of Alcohol: An Islet-Priming Effect." *Diabetes,* Vol. 18 (1969), pp. 517–522.

O'Keefe, S. J. D., and Maris, V. "Lunchtime Gin and Tonic: A Cause for Reactive Hypoglycaemia." *Lancet* (June 8, 1977), pp. 1286–1288.

Serenyi, G., and Endrenyi, L. "Mechanism and Significance of Carbohydrate Intolerance in Chronic Alcoholism." *Metabolism,* Vol. 27, No. 5 (1978), pp. 1041–1046.

3. See Lieber, chapter 5, reference 1.

Bjarnson, I., et al. "The 'Leaky Gut' of Alcoholism: Possible Route of Entry for Toxic Compounds." *Lancet,* Vol. 8370, No. 1 (January 28, 1984) pp. 179–182.

Goldstein, D. B. "Ethanol-Induced Adaptation in Biological Membranes." *Annals of the New York Academy of Science,* Vol. 492 (1987), pp. 103–111.

4. Fraser, R., et al. "Review: The Liver Sinusoidal Cells. Their Role in Disorders of the Liver, Lipoprotein Metabolism, and Atherogenesis." *Pathology,* Vol. 18 (1986), pp. 5–11.

Lieber, C. S. "Metabolic Effects of Ethanol on the Liver and Other Digestive Organs." *Clinics in Gastroenterology,* Vol. 10, No. 2 (1981), pp. 315–342.

5. Bikle, V. K., et al. "Bone Disease in Alcohol Abuse." *Annals of Internal Medicine,* Vol. 103 (1985), pp. 42–48.

6. Petty, F., and Nasrullah, H. A. "Secondary Depression in Alcoholism: Implications for Future Research." *Comprehensive Psychiatry,* Vol. 22 (1981), pp. 587–595.

Keeler, M. H., Taylor, C. I., and Miller, W. C. "Are All Recently Detoxified Alcoholics Depressed?" *American Journal of Psychiatry,* Vol. 136, No. 4B (1979), pp. 586–588.

Weissman, M. M., and Myers, J. K. "Clinical Depression in Alcoholism." *American Journal of Psychiatry,* Vol. 137, No. 3 (1980), pp. 372–373.

7. Asberg, M., et al. "5-HIAAA in the Cerebrospinal Fluid: A Biochemical Suicide Predictor?" *Archives of General Psychiatry,* Vol. 33 (1976), pp. 1193–1197.

Roy, A., et al. "Indices of Serotonin and Glucose Metabolism in Violent Offenders, Arsonists, and Alcoholics." *Annals of the New York Academy of Sciences,* Vol. 487 (1986), pp. 202–220.

Brown, G. L., et al. "Aggression, Suicide, and Serotonin: Relationships to CSF Amine Metabolites." *American Journal of Psychiatry,* Vol. 139, No. 6 (1982), pp. 741–746.

von Knorring, A. L., et al. "Platelet MAO Activity as a Biological Marker in Subgroups of Alcoholism." *Acta Psychiatra Scandanavika,* Vol. 72 (1985), pp. 51–58.

Virkkunen, M. "Reactive Hypoglycemic Tendency among Habitually Violent Offenders." *Neuropsychobiology,* Vol. 8 (1982), pp. 35–40.

8. Yamamoto, H., et al. "Lesions Involving the Suprachiasmatic Nucleus Eliminate the Glucagon Response to Intracranial Injection of 2-deoxy-d-glucose." *Endocrinology,* Vol. 117, No. 2 (1985), pp. 468–473.

9. See Goldstein, chapter 6, reference 3.

10. Lester, B. K., et al. "Chronic Alcoholism, Alcohol, and Sleep," *Alcohol Intoxication and Withdrawal I: Experimental Studies,* ed. M. M. Gross. New York: Plenum Press, 1973, pp. 261–279.

Williams, H. L., and Salamy, A. "Alcohol and Sleep," *The Biology of Alcoholism,* Volume II: *Physiology and Behavior,* eds. B. Kissin and H. Begleiter. New York: Plenum Press, 1973, pp. 435–483.

11. Carpenter, J. A., and Armenti, N. P. "Some Effects of Ethanol on Human Sexual and Aggressive Behavior," *The Biology of Alcoholism*, Volume II: *Physiology and Behavior*, eds. B. Kissin and H. Begleiter. New York: Plenum Press, 1973, pp. 509–543.

12. See reference 3 plus:
Geokas, M. C., et al. "Ethanol, the Liver, and the Gastrointestinal Tract." *Annals of Internal Medicine*, Vol. 95 (1981), pp. 198–211.

13. Sokolow, M. "Heart and Great Vessels," *Current Medical Diagnosis and Treatment*, eds. M. A. Krupp and M. J. Chatton. Los Altos, CA: Lange Medical Publications, 1982, pp. 159–255.
Spillia, R. "Atrial Fibrillation Precipitated by Alcohol." *Lancet* (February 16, 1985), pp. 391–392.
Knott, D. H., and Beard, J. D. "Effects of Alcohol Ingestion on the Cardiovascular System," *Encyclopedic Handbook of Alcoholism*, eds. E. M. Pattison and E. Kaufman. New York: Gardner Press, 1982, pp. 332–342.
Lang, R. M., et al. "Adverse Cardiac Effects of Acute Alcohol Ingestion in Young Adults." *Annals of Internal Medicine*, Vol. 102 (1985), pp. 742–747.

14. Berenyi, M. R., et al. "In Vitro and in Vivo Studies of Cellular Immunity in Alcoholic Cirrhosis." *American Journal of Digestive Diseases*, Vol. 119 (1974), pp. 199–205.
Gluckman, S. J., et al. "Host Defenses during Prolonged Alcohol Consumption in a Controlled Environment." *Archives of Internal Medicine*, Vol. 137 (1977), pp. 1539–1543.
Flavin, D. K. "Alcohol and the Human Immune Defense System." *Medical & Scientific Advisory*, January 20, 1987, National Council on Alcoholism.
Glassman, A. B., et al. "Effects of Ethyl Alcohol on Human Peripheral Lymphocytes." *Archives of Pathology and Laboratory Medicine*, Vol. 109 (1985), pp. 540–542.

MacGregor, R. R. "Alcohol and Immune Defense." *Journal of the American Medical Association,* Vol. 256, No. 1 (1986), pp. 1474–1479.

Nouri-Aria, K. T., et al. "To and B Cell Function in Alcoholic Liver Disease." *Journal of Hepatology,* Vol. 2 (1986), pp. 195–207.

Rajkovic, I. A., and Williams, R. "Mechanisms of Abnormalities in Host Defenses against Bacterial Infection in Liver Disease." *Clinical Science,* Vol. 68 (1985), pp. 247–253.

15. Lieber, C. S., et al. "Alcohol-Related Diseases and Carcinogenesis." *Cancer Research,* Vol. 39 (1979), pp. 2863–2886.

16. See Bjarnason, et al. and Goldstein, reference 3.

Mayron, L. W. "Portals of Entry—A Review." *Annals of Allergy,* Vol. 40, No. 6 (1978), pp. 399–405.

17. Sugerman, A. A., et al. "A Study of Antibody Levels in Alcoholic, Depressive, and Schizophrenic Patients." *Annals of Allergy,* Vol. 48 (1982), pp. 166–171.

Closson, W. "Levels of IgE Antibodies in Hospitalized Alcoholics vs. Nonalcoholic Elective Surgery Controls." Unpublished paper, Brunswick Hospital Center, NY, 1985.

18. Lieber, C. S. "Biochemical and Molecular Basis of Alcohol-Induced Injury to Liver and Other Tissues." *The New England Journal of Medicine,* Vol. 319, No. 25 (1988), pp. 1639–1650.

Hoerner, M., et al. "The Role of Alcoholism and Liver Disease in the Appearance of Serum Antibodies against Acetaldehyde Adducts." *Hepatology,* Vol. 8 (1988), pp. 569–574.

7. Withdrawal

1. The data on alcoholism withdrawal and its treatment are extensive throughout the medical literature. In developing this chapter I

made extensive use of the materials issued by the American Society for Addiction Medicine, as well as my own years of clinical experience.

8. The Dilemma of Diagnosis—Doctors

1. Clare, A. W. "Alcohol Education and the Medical Student." *Alcohol and Alcoholism,* Vol. 19, No. 4 (1984), pp. 291–296.
Whitfield, C. L. "Medical Education and Alcoholism." *Maryland State Medical Journal,* Vol. 29, No. 10 (1980), pp. 77–83.

2. Lisansky, L. T. "Why Physicians Avoid Early Diagnosis of Alcoholism." *New York State Journal of Medicine* (September 1975), pp. 1788–1792.

3. The Johns Hopkins project was described by Joseph Levine in the February 1988 issue of *Johns Hopkins Magazine* (p. 13–20). The project, which has been in existence since 1984, takes a two-pronged approach to the problem of mis- and underdiagnosis of alcoholism. On the ward, department leaders and alcoholism leaders try to increase the awareness of house staff, while in the medical school, courses on alcoholism have been added and updated.

9. Identifying the Alcoholic

1. Selzer, M. E. "The Michigan Alcoholism Screening Test: The Quest for a New Diagnostic Instrument." *American Journal of Psychiatry,* Vol. 127, No. 2 (1971), pp. 1653–1658. The MAST was developed in the late sixties as a "consistent, quantifiable, structured interview instrument for the detection of alcoholism." It has proved to be a fairly accurate tool for quickly identifying the person with alcoholism in hospital situations. It is, however, meant to be administered directly to patients with suspected alcoholism (not their friends or relatives), and clinical confirmation (blood tests, etc.) is advisable.

10. The Dilemma of Diagnosis—Patients and Families

1. Mapes, B.E., et al. "The Alcoholic Family: Diagnosis and Treatment." *Alcoholism Treatment Quarterly*, Vol. 1, No. 4 (1984), pp. 67–83.

2. Steinglass, P. "Family Therapy in Alcoholism," *The Biology of Alcoholism*, vol. 5: *Treatment and Rehabilitation of the Chronic Alcoholic* (B. Kissin and H. Begleiter, eds.) New York: Plenum Press, 1977, pp. 259–299.

3. Schaef, A. W.: *Co-Dependence: Misunderstood—Misdiagnosed.* Minneapolis, MN: Winston Press, 1986.

11. Getting into Treatment

1. The intervention techniques described in this chapter are an amalgam of information found in various Al-Anon publications and the actual clinical and personal experiences of myself and my colleagues at Brunswick House. For further information on Al-Anon, see chapter 17.

12. Choosing a Treatment Program

1. The recommended criteria for a treatment program are a combination of my own clinical experience and the guidelines for diagnosis and treatment set forth by the American Society for Addiction Medicine (ASAM). Many facilities do not place as much emphasis on biological evaluation and rehabilitation. They should be avoided. Conversely, any facility that does not provide a full range of counseling (including family counseling), education, and behavioral retraining should also be avoided. A comprehensive and balanced program is essential.

13. Long-Term Recovery—Getting High and Staying that Way

1. Sobell, M. B. and Sobell, L. C. *Behavioral Treatment of Alcoholism.* New York: Plenum Press, 1978.

Pendery, M.L., et al. "Controlled Drinking by Alcoholics? New Findings and a Reevaluation of a Major Affirmative Study." *Science,* Vol. 217 (1982), pp. 169–175.

The issue of "controlled" or "moderate" drinking has been a matter of debate for nearly three decades. Between 1970 and 1971, the Sobells (of Patton State Hospital in California) trained twenty patients with alcoholism to practice controlled drinking. Controlled drinking was defined as drinking only mixed drinks, sipping these drinks, pacing them at least twenty minutes apart and setting a moderate cutoff point. All twenty patients had shown physical dependence with lack of control over their drinking. A matched group of twenty patients were treated with the goal of abstinence. All forty were male.

The Sobells reported that the controlled drinking group functioned significantly better, with fewer serious adverse effects (jail, hospitalization, etc.) than the other group over a two-year period. A third year follow-up by another group of researchers confirmed their findings.

Ten years later, another group of researchers (Pendery et al.) investigated the status of the twenty controlled drinking subjects to determine whether controlled drinking was a desirable or attainable long-term goal. Their findings were quite different.

Thirteen of the subjects who had been considered functioning well had been readmitted within one year of their initial discharge. Two subjects were readmitted within two weeks. Six others lasted four months. The average time before readmission was approximately five months. Of the thirteen, four were readmitted suffering from delirium tremens. Two were suicidal. One had become violent and beaten his wife. Another was cross-addicted to tranquilizers and had been for five years (although no mention was made of this in the original study).

In all, of the twenty controlled drinkers: "Only one, who apparently had not experienced physical withdrawal symptoms, maintained a pattern of controlled drinking. Eight continued to drink excessively—regularly or intermittently—despite repeated damaging consequences; six abandoned their efforts to engage in controlled drinking and became abstinent; four died from alcohol-related causes; and one, certified about a year after discharge from the research project as gravely disabled because of drinking, was missing."

The findings illustrate the essential fallacy of controlled drinking. The person with alcoholism is not capable of "controlling" his or her drinking, and there is absolutely no reliable research or clinical evidence to support "moderate" drinking in these patients.

2. The listing of alcohol content of common medications is part of an information packet for the recovering alcoholic that is given to all patients being discharged from Brunswick House.

3. The behavioral guidelines for continued sobriety are based on actual instructions developed by Geraldine Owen Delaney, Chief Executive Officer of Alina Lodge.

Larsen, E. *Stage Two Recovery: Life Beyond Addiction.* San Francisco: Harper & Row, 1985.

4. The Twelve Steps and the Twelve Traditions are from *Alcoholics Anonymous* (The Big Book), 3d edition, the basic text for Alcoholics Anonymous. It can be purchased from: Alcoholics Anonymous World Services, Inc., Box 459, Grand Central Station, New York, NY 10163.

14. Prevention—Don't Let It Happen to You

1. The information in this chapter was culled from my own years of clinical work, as well as the knowledge and experience of my

colleagues at Brunswick House. Some of the prevention guidelines are also the result of interviews with members of Students Against Driving Drunk (SADD), as well as a review of Al-Anon/Alateen literature. Contact information on both SADD and Alateen can be found in chapter 17. Additional thanks to Phyllis Ozarin of Recovery Resources for information on the syndrome of codependence.

15. Other Drugs

1. Beasley, J. D. *Diagnosing and Managing Chemical Dependency.* Dallas: Essential Medical Information Systems, 1989.

2. Weil, A., and Rosen, W. *Chocolate to Morphine: Understanding Mind-Active Drugs.* Boston: Houghton Mifflin, 1983.

FOR FURTHER READING

Biology and Genetics

Beasley, Joseph D., M.D. *Wrong Diagnosis, Wrong Treatment: The Plight of the Alcoholic in America.* Dallas: Essential Medical Information Systems, 1987.

Goodwin, Donald, M.D. *Is Alcoholism Hereditary?* New York: Oxford University Press, 1976.

Milam, James R., and Katherine Ketcham. *Under the Influence: A Guide to the Myths and Realities of Alcoholism.* Seattle: Madrona Publishers, 1981.

Alcohol and Health (Sixth Special Report to the U.S. Congress from the secretary of health and human services). Rockville, MD: U.S. Dept. of Health and Human Services, 1987.

Nutrition

Barkie, Karen E. *Sweet and SugarFree: An All-Natural, Fruit-Sweetened Dessert Cookbook.* New York: St. Martin's Press, 1982.

Goldbeck, Nikki and David. *The Supermarket Handbook: Access to Whole Foods.* New York: Signet Books, 1976.

Ketcham, Katherine, and L. Ann Mueller, M.D. *Eating Right to Live Sober.* Seattle: Madrona Publishers, 1983.

Williams, Roger, Ph.D. *The Prevention of Alcoholism Through Nutrition.* New York: Bantam Books, 1981.

Other Drugs

Weil, Andrew, M.D., and Winifred Rosen. *Chocolate to Morphine: Understanding Mind-Active Drugs.* New York: Houghton Mifflin Co., 1983.

Resolving Psychological/Emotional Issues

Wegsheider-Cruse, Sharon. *Adult Children of Alcoholics: A Guide to Recovery.*

Schaeff, Anne Wilson. *Co-Dependence: Misunderstood—Mistreated.* Minneapolis, MN: Winston Press, 1986.

Larsen, Earnie. *Stage II Recovery: Life Beyond Addiction.* San Francisco: Harper & Row, 1985.

Whitfield, Charles L. *Healing the Child Within.* Deerfield Beach, FL: Health Communications, Inc., 1987.

INDEX

ABOUT THE AUTHOR

Joseph D. Beasley, M.D., is a board-certified clinician practicing in the field of alcoholism and chemical dependency. He is Medical Director of Brunswick House in Amityville, Long Island, the largest private alcoholism treatment facility in New York State. He is a member of the American Society of Addiction Medicine, and has been certified by examination as a specialist in addiction medicine by the society. A former department head at Harvard University, chairman of the Planned Parenthood Federation of American, dean of the School of Public Health at Tulane University, and member of the National Commission of Population Growth and the American Future, Dr. Beasley is now the director of the Institute of Health Policy and Practice of the Bard College Center. He is the author of *Wrong Diagnosis, Wrong Treatment: The Plight of the Alcoholic in America,* and *Diagnosing and Managing Chemical Dependency,* as well as a monthly column on chemical dependency for *The Medical Tribune.*